C000282916

The Jungle

The Jungle
Calais's Camps and Migrants

Michel Agier

With Yasmine Bouagga, Maël Galisson,
Cyrille Hanappe, Mathilde Pette
and Philippe Wannesson

With the collaboration of Madeleine Trépanier,
Céline Barré, Nicolas Lambert, Sara Prestianni
and Julien Saison

Translated by David Fernbach

polity

Copyright © Michel Agier, Yasmine Bouagga, Maël Galisson, Cyrille Hanappe, Mathilde Pette and Philippe Wannesson, 2019

This English edition © Polity Press, 2019

Polity Press
65 Bridge Street
Cambridge CB2 1UR, UK

Polity Press
101 Station Landing
Suite 300
Medford, MA 02155, USA

All rights reserved. Except for the quotation of short passages for the purpose of criticism and review, no part of this publication may be reproduced, stored in a retrieval system or transmitted, in any form or by any means, electronic, mechanical, photocopying, recording or otherwise, without the prior permission of the publisher.

ISBN-13: 978-1-5095-3060-1
ISBN-13: 978-1-5095-3061-8 (pb)

A catalogue record for this book is available from the British Library.

Library of Congress Cataloging-in-Publication Data

Names: Agier, Michel, 1953- author.
Title: The jungle : Calais's camps and migrants / Michel Agier et al.
Description: 1 | Medford, MA : Polity, 2018. | Includes bibliographical references and
  index.
Identifiers: LCCN 2018013003 (print) | LCCN 2018029163 (ebook) | ISBN
  9781509530632 (Epub) | ISBN 9781509530601 (hardback) | ISBN 9781509530618
  (paperback)
Subjects: LCSH: Political refugees–France–Calais. | Refuge (Humanitarian assistance)–
  France–Calais. | BISAC: SOCIAL SCIENCE / Anthropology / General.
Classification: LCC HV677.C342 (ebook) | LCC HV677.C342 A45 2018 (print) |
  DDC 362.89/912830944272–dc23
LC record available at https://lccn.loc.gov/2018013003

Typeset in 10.5 on 12 pt Sabon
by Toppan Best-set Premedia Limited
Printed and bound in Great Britain by Clays Ltd, Elcograf S.p.A.

The publisher has used its best endeavours to ensure that the URLs for external websites referred to in this book are correct and active at the time of going to press. However, the publisher has no responsibility for the websites and can make no guarantee that a site will remain live or that the content is or will remain appropriate.

Every effort has been made to trace all copyright holders, but if any have been inadvertently overlooked the publisher will be pleased to include any necessary credits in any subsequent reprint or edition.

For further information on Polity, visit our website:
politybooks.com

Contents

Illustrations

Photos

Figures

Maps

Introduction: for a better understanding

On 24 October 2016, the evacuation of the Calais Jungle began. The relevant department of the French interior ministry and the police, along with members of various voluntary organizations, led the occupants of the shantytown camp to coaches that would take them to reception centres whose names and locations they did not know. In the first three days, a little more than 3,000 people were moved in this way. On the third day, the destruction of dwellings began, and also of the communal facilities built during the previous eighteen months of occupation and installation. At the end of the same week, the government authorities announced that the 'dismantling' was finished. In fact, the complete destruction would still take a few more days. Left until last were the containers that the government had decided to place in the middle of the Jungle nearly a year earlier. These were taken apart and removed a few weeks later.

The demolition of the Jungle was seen as a success. It took place at the start of a major election campaign in France (the presidential elections of April and May 2017), in which the existing government sought (without success) to win back an electorate that it had very largely lost. To this end it wanted to show signs of its 'firmness' and 'humanity', in the official 'elements of language'. Above all, the state sought to demonstrate its ability to suppress the public problem posed by the migrants, through the disappearance of the migrants themselves along with any trace of their local presence, their settlement on the ground. This would be the signal of a strong state, protecting the national territory against undesirable foreigners.

A longer history of the Jungle

And yet, only a few months later, at the end of January 2017, the national press as well as voluntary organizations acknowledged that migrants were still at Calais. Those who had been unwilling to take the coaches the previous October had dispersed in the region around the town and were now coming back, while others returned from further away, after realizing that the reception centres (Centres d'Accueil et d'Orientation [Reception and Orientation Centres], or CAOs) to which they had been taken when the Jungle was demolished were a dead end, since they neither resolved the administrative obstacles to their asylum requests nor succeeded in making them abandon the attempt to cross to Britain. Thus the history of the Calais migrants did not finish with the 'eviction' of October 2016 (studied in detail in chapter 5). The story that needs to be told is a much longer one – in its historical and geographical context, European and regional – just as we have to understand what happened in this shantytown – or rather a town and a community in the process of coming together – that the whole world called 'the Jungle', and where, at least at one point, 10,000 people lived. What crazy mechanisms enabled Europe, and in particular France and the United Kingdom, to 'invent' and 'manufacture', then destroy, this unnameable place? So unnameable that fear was further intensified by calling it a 'Jungle', taking up, distorting and above all re-signifying the Pashtun word *djangal* (which, in its original language, simply means a bit of forest) so as to Westernize it a bit, and thus designate it from this point of view, French and European, as a negatively exotic and disturbing place, more distant than it is in reality, and less human.

What the present book describes is the very opposite of this. Based on a chronological and monographic study conducted by a team that included researchers, students and members of voluntary organizations,[1] it offers points of reference to help understand what has been happening at Calais for the last fifteen years and more – and has continued since the demolition of the camp and the dispersal of its occupants. Also the book describes and analyses what happened in the Jungle itself between April 2015 and October 2016, the respective dates of the opening of the encampment and of its destruction. The overall context of the Jungle is what has been called in Europe the 'migrant crisis'. But the causal connection between the formation and development of this site and the so-called migrant crisis is only very indirect. What is taking place on the Franco–British border has its origin in the 1990s. It is important to place this situation in an older local and regional context: that of Europe's external borders since 1995 and the establishment of the Schengen space (connected also with the borders at Ceuta, Melilla and Patras – see map 1). At the same time, to take Calais as a case study means describing an example of the European crisis in general.

The closing of the Sangatte camp in 2002 (the emergency shelter and reception centre of the Red Cross, 1999–2002)

Map 1. The Schengen area.

was already supposed to mean, according to the French government of the time, that 'there will be no more crossing at Calais'. However, thousands of migrants of different generations and nationalities (Kosovars, Kurds, Afghans, Eritreans, Sudanese, Iraqis, Syrians, etc.) continued to wander in the region between Calais and Dunkirk. They tried to cross to the UK despite the Franco–British agreement on keeping migrants on French territory, made at Le Touquet in 2003. The formation of the Calais encampment – also called a 'state shantytown' or the 'New Jungle' when it was created in April 2015 – was just one episode in this long border history, and certainly a singular one, in the context of the exceptional arrival of a million migrants in Europe that year. From Lesbos to Calais, Idomeni to Ventimiglia, hundreds of encampments, reception and holding centres, 'hot spots' and other sites of confinement developed as never before around Europe's borders, in its margins and even at the heart of its cities.[2]

Europe and the migration question

The policy of removing undesirable immigrants began twenty-five years earlier, with the 'Schengen process', whose regulations centred on taking measures to prevent their entry into this territory. The European Council meeting held at Tampere in October 1999, which started the process of harmonizing policies in this field, saw the appearance of the concept of 'external action' or 'externalization', as well as 'partnership with the countries of origin', which would lead in the following years to a policy of subcontracting the management of migration and asylum to countries in Africa and the Middle East. The concept of externalization reappeared in the agenda of a meeting at The Hague in October 2004 (which set the programme and objectives for European asylum and immigration policy for the following five years), as well as in the proposal of Tony Blair's government that centres for sorting asylum requests should be set up in the countries around the European Union. The following years brought the question of control and criminalization of migrants to the heart of European policy, to the detriment of integration and reception. The March 2016 agreement between the EU and Turkey represents one of the latest examples of the drift in European policy, externalization of border control to third countries being a central pillar of this. Moreover, at the level of member states, emergency management not only substitutes for any real long-term planning, but also for genuine measures that would reduce deaths at sea, which are tragically rising every year.[3]

The year 2015 was marked by an increase in the number of refugees entering European territory. The figure reached over a million individuals. There then followed a brief period in which the determination of these refugees, combined with the interests of certain member states, made it possible to reverse the trend and create what would be known as the 'Balkan corridor', which offered a safe and rapid passage for refugees from Greece towards Austria and Germany. But this corridor began to close in November 2015, when at Idomeni, on the border between Macedonia and Greece, an arbitrary sorting of entries began, allowing only individuals of Syrian and Iraqi nationality to cross.

Early in 2016 this border closed completely, at the same time as did the entire Balkan corridor (the Greece—Macedonia—Serbia—Hungary (or Croatia/Slovenia)—Austria route). The refugees who continued to arrive in Greece, chiefly across the Aegean Sea, remained boxed in on Greek territory, in reception camps opened by the government under pressure from the EU ('hot spots'), where conditions were inhumane, or in makeshift camps around the borders, such as those that formed at Idomeni and Piraeus. The signing of the agreement between the EU and Turkey on 18 March 2016 went in the same direction of closure. In exchange for a faster process of visa issue for Turkish citizens, as well as €6 billion, Turkey committed itself to controlling its borders and readmitting to its territory those asylum seekers on the Greek islands who were considered non-admissible. If arrivals on mainland Greece significantly diminished in the wake of this agreement, the Greek islands, and particularly Lesbos, were transformed into a real limbo, where thousands of people waited months without knowing their fate.

Calais is simply one step in a migration journey that lasts months, even years, and obliges the refugees to seek shelter – in the absence of genuine reception policies – in makeshift encampments scattered right across Europe, whether at Calais, Rome, Ventimiglia, Paris, Idomeni, Subotica, Patras or elsewhere.

At Calais there are both people who crossed to Sicily, and those who entered overland or by sea to Greece.

Those landing in Sicily – chiefly refugees from sub-Saharan Africa or the Horn of Africa – have very often suffered extremely severe violence and conditions of life before reaching Europe. In Mali, Niger or Sudan, the attempt to reach Libya begins in the ghettos of Gao, Agadez and Khartoum, with people often imprisoned before they start on the desert crossing in a truck weighed down with its human cargo, those weakened by the journey and without the strength to continue being simply left on the sand. Libya, which has made migrants into a real money-spinner, is where all who cross it suffer the greatest violence: often kidnapped on their arrival, at Koufra or Sebha, imprisoned in dozens of holding centres scattered across the country before being exploited as cheap labour. The Libyan transit is still harder for women, victims of violence on the part of the authorities and military who control the territory. After having survived the test of the Mediterranean Sea, and despite being obliged to identify themselves – particularly after the 'hot spot' controls established in September 2015 – many refugees decide to leave Italy for another European country.

The Tiburtina station in Rome is the meeting-point for refugees from the Horn of Africa, travelling from Sicily to the borders of Ventimiglia and Como. Those seeking to reach France or specifically Calais continue to Ventimiglia, those set on Switzerland or Germany head for Como or Bolzano. The policy of closing borders even within the Schengen space has led to the creation of informal or temporary camps managed by the Red Cross, where migrants await the aid of a smuggler[4] to continue their journey.

Whether referred to as 'migrants' or 'refugees', the inhabitants of the Calais shantytown share a common experience of displacement from their country of origin, with the aim of settling in a place where they might find protection and a perspective for the future. The migrants at Calais were those among the individuals crossing Europe who hoped to reach the UK (where they often have relatives or an already established community, or think they have a greater chance of integration), but found themselves blocked at the border. Between 2014 and 2016, the number of migrants in the makeshift encampments around the crossing points to England grew to unprecedented levels, due both to the growing number of refugees entering the European Union and to the reinforcement of the UK border.

The main nationalities present were Afghans and Sudanese, who in 2016 made up more than two-thirds of the total number of migrants on the site. The population of migrants at Calais reflects a certain state of conflicts in the world, yet it is not an exact representation of the migrant populations reaching Europe during this period, nor even of those arriving illegally across the Mediterranean. Whereas on Lesbos the majority are Syrians, there are only a few of these at Calais, since they tend more to favour Germany or the Scandinavian countries. Likewise, the migrants from Francophone Africa, who are numerous among those arriving on the Italian shores, are almost absent at Calais, not wishing to seek asylum in the UK. Only a minority of individuals seeking refuge in Europe are blocked at Calais. Besides, depending on the routes taken from their country of origin, the demographic weight of nationalities shifts. The EU–Turkey agreement and the blocking of the Balkan route in spring 2016 reduced the number of Afghans, Syrians and Kurds arriving. Conversely, the seasonal reopening of the Italian Mediterranean route led to a sharp increase in the proportion of Sudanese, Eritreans and Ethiopians during the course of summer 2016.

Calais as metonym for European crisis … and solidarity

Calais represents one staging-post on a trajectory of migration that is often long – anything from several weeks to several years – in the course of which displaced individuals are blocked at several political and geographical border crossings. The double obstacle of a stretch of sea 30 kilometres wide, and a border where security was reinforced in 2015, made Calais a cul-de-sac where the temporary became permanent, where the encampment ended up persisting and even urbanizing. This transformation, paradoxically, also made it a staging-post for many refugees seeking asylum in France. From a place of transit to England, the Calais shantytown thus became, throughout the 2015–16 period, a relatively hospitable site for migrants of various status, given the lack of public arrangements for reception and transit adapted to their situation in France.

Calais – a border town of the Schengen space, a place of transit to an England whose borders are increasingly externalized and securitized. The refugees find it a temporary refuge, while waiting either to cross or to make an asylum application in France. Calais is a town with multiple borders, where not only European policies are tried out, but also national and municipal ones, policies of reception and rejection of migrant and refugee populations.

Viewed as a transit space not only by migrants but also by institutions and the local population, Calais is one of the most constricting national spaces in terms of security and the eviction of foreigners from the urban space. But this temporary transit zone has turned out to be increasingly durable, on account of the reinforcement of border controls and the establishment of a physical border (barbed-wire fences) at the crossing points (port and tunnel).

The creation of the camp, officially known as 'campement de la Lande' [i.e., Heath camp], corresponded to a public strategy of management of the migrant populations outside of the town. It was initiated by voluntary organizations and individuals who saw it as a way of improving the living conditions of refugees on this new site. Situated 7 kilometres from the town of Calais, and 34 kilometres from England, at the heart of a border zone that is closed and controlled by a Franco–British security system, the Calais camp was first and foremost a site of extraterritoriality.

The transfer and regrouping of migrants and refugees into a single 'tolerated' camp, some distance from the town, took place in April 2015, as a response of the French state to the request of the Calais mayor (a member of the main right-wing party, Les Républicains). This led to a new sequence of tensions and outbreaks of violence, but also gestures of solidarity, social, media and political mobilizations, which made Calais a metonym for Europe's crisis in the face of the influx of migrants from Africa, Asia and the Middle East, but also for a Europe of solidarity, more open to others and the world.

This solidarity also gave rise to major intellectual mobilizations. Many books have been published in both French and English on the subject of migrants and the Calais Jungle, which shows the particular place that this situation rapidly acquired, not only in the domain of research, but also in political and artistic action. By its dynamism and its art of transformation, as much as by its marginality and precariousness, the Calais Jungle rapidly stimulated thought. By way of personal visits, 'philosophical reportage' or longer-lasting investigations, philosophers found here material for renewing their reflections on (in)hospitality, citizenship, cosmopolitanism, globalization, the status of foreigners and national public policies in the face of precarious mobility.[5] Other works have taken the form of manifestos, artistic, poetic and political actions, some of these issuing from the 'Appel des 800'.[6] These are original expressions based on various kinds of writing or testimony: photographic, film, literary, philosophical, cartoons, and publications of the words and writings of migrants.[7]

We have followed closely these voices and mobilizations, and integrated them into our diagnosis of 'what happened at Calais' – the Calais event. They help us to understand how a place created to make its occupants as invisible as possible, as close to disappearing altogether, became, without losing hardly anything of its precariousness (in other words, with the possibility of disappearance a constant throughout), a site of life and very great visibility, the theatre of new political, urban and aesthetic questions for Europeans.

The present work, however, differs from those just mentioned in the sense that it is first and foremost a research document and an archive of the present. Without needing the form of an indictment, it offers a collective anthropological expertise, a procedure which could be called 'forensic anthropology' if this expression did not refer too closely to an outdated biological and physical conception of anthropology. It is forensic in the sense of forensic medicine – investigating the causes and processes that lead to the death of an individual. But this is social, cultural and political anthropology, applied to a place, communities, a situation. This book thus presents a diagnosis of the causes, process and effects of the life and death of the Calais Jungle (April 2015 to October 2016). The detailed descriptions and analyses conducted as closely as possible on the ground seek both to establish what happened at Calais and to draw more general lessons. Our desire is to produce knowledge on the basis of this case, from the perspective of an anthropology of contemporary dynamics and using the method of 'extended case study' developed by field anthropologists of the Manchester School.[8] This method makes it possible to grasp and retain moments of a world in constant transformation. Starting from a particular situation, localized in space and time, the aim is to draw out all the threads for understanding the logics that 'produced' this situation and thereby understand a more global change under way, a new state of societies – both local and global – coming about and being steadily transformed, with the stakes and perspectives that arise from this.

Anthropology has to be reactive, collective, and multidisciplinary, in order to meet the 'contemporaneity' between research and the perpetual motion of the present. A whole team has been mobilized to achieve this work, and we draw on historical, architectural and urban, sociological and political research, as well as on ethnography and participation in the field. The study has thus gained from being collaborative, bringing together those engaged in fieldwork and members of voluntary organizations who met on the ground, with several years' familiarity with the site (and those that preceded it), who were determined to draw from their experience an archive and a body of knowledge. More broadly, it forms part of an attempt to renew anthropological research and writing in the project of understanding in depth the transformations under way in the contemporary world.

As a first-hand research document, this book is addressed to everyone wishing to understand the situation and its context in detail. It is also the history of a present that is still being made, since it is concerned with both the pre- and post-Jungle experience. Throughout the text, we are equally careful not to isolate Calais from its regional environment – and particularly to mention the town of Grand-Synthe, some 40 kilometres away, where a very different municipal experience developed. Calais is one place of encampment/

camp/shantytown among others in the north of France, in Europe, and in the world. These various sites are linked, they form networks, and enable us to reach a wider conception of the name of Calais, of what Calais signifies, as 'concentrate' of a change on the global scale, on a planet where extra-territoriality and policies of exception are spreading.

Keeping as precisely as possible to the chronology of some twenty years of migration policies and population movements that led to the opening, and eighteen months later the destruction, of the Calais Jungle, we describe in parallel movements of solidarity and hostility. The seemingly major local role of the far right (much has been said about how 'the Calais people' were 'xenophobic') is put in its proper place, almost derisory in relation to the hostility of the public authorities (municipal and national) to the migrants. Conversely, local movements of solidarity towards migrants developed substantially from the early 2000s, and played an important role in making it possible for migrants to live here despite the hostile context. We also dwell on the spatial and social forms that were invented during these years of wandering through the Calais squats and encampments up to this final site – which was first called the 'New Jungle' – showing that all these installations enjoyed a relative autonomy – an unforeseen and inverted consequence of their removal by the public authorities.

The first chapter offers a detailed and contextualized chronology of the events that led to the formation of the camp (in April 2015) and then its destruction (October 2016). This falls into four main phases: from the 1980s to the 'Sangatte moment' (1999–2002); then the post-Sangatte period until 2015, for which we describe the rise of both the far right and movements of solidarity; the formation and development of the Calais camp in 2015; and finally the period from its partial destruction of March 2016 to its total destruction and the dispersal of the migrants in October 2016. This history has been reconstructed with the help of interviews and existing documentation, but above all thanks to the archive constituted by the memories of members of voluntary organizations, who, as co-authors of this book with their personal reflections, sought both to bear witness to the period 1999–2016 and to understand it.

The book then pursues a descriptive, reflective and critical approach, taking the case of the Calais Jungle to draw three main 'lessons' (chapters 2, 3 and 4). These bear on the basic questions for understanding the new models of mobility and locality on the European and global scale. The first lesson (chapter 2) concerns the infrastructure of sites of mobility. This chapter develops an architectural and town-planning perspective, describing the transformation and improvement of the spaces created by the migrants in the urban encampments and the Calais camp itself, where an encampment architecture and a precarious town-planning were invented: a 'draft' for a town, provoking wider reflection on receptive urbanism in contexts of mobility. The second lesson (chapter 3) is a sociology of life in precarious conditions. This chapter focuses on the everyday routine in the Calais Jungle in 2015 and 2016. Transformed into a shantytown, a real urban laboratory, it became a relatively hospitable site in a political context of official hostility. The consequences of this reflection also bear on the question of hospitality at the level of towns and the social self-organization of precarious sites, the place and representations of urban marginality in the rich countries: what were the values and the urban model in terms of which the Calais Jungle was considered 'undignified'? The third lesson focuses on the confrontation between government policies to reject migrants and refugees, and movements of solidarity from inhabitants at the local and European level (chapter 4). This solidarity facilitated a transformation, however tiny it might seem, of local European societies and the place that foreign migrants occupy in them. We counterpose the way towns react to migrants (in some places rejection, in others welcome) with the way migrants act towards the town and its more settled inhabitants. From a generic and abstract fear of the Other, to a relationship with the Other who is here, has a name, exchanges knowledge and continues to learn, the town of Calais and its camp always speak to us of reciprocity. Finally, we devote a chapter to describing the demolition of the shantytown camp between 24 and 31 October 2016, which became the object of a media and political circus in the French pre-election context, as well as the beginnings of a return to the site that could be observed a few months later. By way of conclusion, we come back to the meaning of the Calais event as political, media and symbolic object. In fact, all the indignation directed at the Jungle, all the physical and moral violence against its inhabitants, and all the types of solidarity (humanitarian and political, from individuals and voluntary associations, Calais locals, British and Europeans), form a concentrate of questions that are asked right across Europe today: how is a local, national and European 'we' defined, that posits its relationship with Others and with itself? What place does it provide for foreigners, migrants or refugees? Is it possible to reinvent hospitality on the basis of the camps or against them, and if so, how? What future is being imagined in these places of distancing and exception, which end up resembling occupations and new political spaces?

1

Movement to and fro: the Calais region from 1986 to 2016

In 1986, Amnesty International focused on the situation of persons rejected at the UK border who found themselves homeless in Calais and without resources. Some of them seemed to be covered by the Geneva Convention on Refugees, and should thus have been able to request asylum. Under the impulse of Amnesty International, some inhabitants of Calais took up this question. That was the origin of La Belle Étoile [The Beautiful Star], formed in 1994. It is impossible to say, thirty years later, whether it was by chance that this organization set up to defend human rights was aware at that point of a phenomenon which was not completely new (the rejection of migrants at the UK border), or if a reinforcement of border controls and a tightening of the rules governing entry to British territory made these individuals more numerous and more visible.

At that time, the rules of entry to European countries were generally far more flexible than they are today, and it was much easier to enter legally. The number of people affected by these rejections was therefore low. The Calais story is less one of an increasing migration than of a border that became closed to certain populations, coming chiefly, though not exclusively, from dictatorships and countries at war.

Moreover, UK border control was then carried out on the other side of the Channel, on English soil. The Channel

Tunnel did not exist. The port was not yet surrounded by fences, and the train took travellers to the ferry terminal, where they only had to pass through the French customs.

That was thirty years ago. The intervening period has been marked by alternate periods of high visibility and relative disregard. Attention is drawn by individuals and particularly their congregation, by encampments, squats, shantytowns, 'jungles' or institutional camps, to the point of relegating to the background the causes of the situation under our eyes. Moments of high visibility call for action on the part of the public authorities, who, finding themselves in the spotlight, offer some measures that attract attention, and others, sometimes just as important, that pass unnoticed. Calais was the focus of attention, although the situation is far more widespread, along the coastline from Brittany to the Netherlands, and now also from Spain to Germany, inland along the axes of communication, and in Paris, which has become rather a 'suburb of Calais' in this respect.

1986–1997: the indifference of the French authorities

La Belle Étoile, the first organization of support for migrants blocked or rejected at the border, gave them material help and legal aid. To this end it worked with other voluntary organizations, such as Cimade and France Terre d'Asile [France Land of Asylum], or with public services such as the Service Social d'Aide aux Étrangers [Social Service for Assistance to Foreigners] and the Centres d'Hébergement et de Réinsertion Sociale [Shelter and Social Reintegration Centres]. A British organization, Migrant Helpline, contacted it when vulnerable individuals were rejected at Dover in an attempt to enter the UK.

The public authorities were not particularly concerned about the situation at this time, either in the sense of support or of hostility and a repressive response to the migrants' presence. It was possible to appeal to existing frameworks of common law or support for foreigners.

Certain situations were particularly complex, such as that of individuals rejected by the UK whom the French authorities refused to readmit to French territory. Some people found themselves travelling back and forth on the ferries between the two border controls before their situation was resolved. Since then, agreements on readmission make it obligatory for the country that the person is coming from to readmit them to its territory if they are refused admission to the neighbouring country.

From 1990, with the fall of the Communist regimes, citizens of East European countries were able to travel to EU territory without a visa. However, they were frequently rejected at the UK border, and soon found themselves blocked at Calais. These were often groups travelling by bus, who had to await the return of the bus to go back to their home country. Sometimes several dozen people found themselves sleeping in a ferry terminal, lacking money for a hotel room or the fare home. This situation was not taken into account by either the state services or the municipality.

The opening of the Channel Tunnel in 1994 created a new underground border between France and the UK. Symbolically, for one section of British opinion, this connection between Great Britain and the continent put an end to British insularity and the security this permitted. The Sangatte protocol, signed in 1991, addressed this concern with a symbolic response. It organized the control of this new border, stipulating that control of entry into the UK would be carried out in France before entering the Tunnel. Symmetrically, French controls would take place in the UK, and this measure had a practical effect in terms of the fluidity of traffic. But it was also the first step in a policy of externalization of UK border control measures on French soil, which would become increasingly asymmetrical. The protocol was supplemented in 1993 by a tripartite agreement between Belgium, France and the UK concerning trains originating in Brussels and using the Channel Tunnel.

1997–1999: a growing attention

From the late 1990s, the two neighbouring states, France and the UK, would increasingly coordinate their response to the situation of migrants blocked or rejected at the UK border.

On 13 October 1997, a group of Roma from the Czech Republic and Slovakia requested asylum from the British authorities. Their application was rejected, and they were returned to France. These forty people then found themselves sleeping in the ferry terminal at Calais. A month later, under pressure from La Belle Étoile, the prefecture of the Pas-de-Calais department agreed to requisition a building near the port to accommodate them. It would still take two months for the French and British governments to agree a solution to their administrative situation. Half of the families were authorized to enter the UK and apply for asylum, while the other half made their asylum applications in France.

In 1998 and 1999, the number of people arriving rose sharply, particularly with the war in Kosovo. There would sometimes be up to a hundred people sleeping in the ferry terminal, including a growing number of families. The context at Calais became tougher. The Centres d'Hébergement et de Réinsertion Sociale were ever more reticent to accept migrants, as were local hotels, and the voluntary organizations had increasing difficulty in finding places for migrants to stay.

On 23 April 1999, a decree by the prefect banned overnight stays in the ferry terminal, at the request of the Chambre de Commerce et d'Industrie, which managed the port: 'any use of the public sections of the Calais Cross-Channel Terminal for purposes other than the traffic of travellers is FORBID-DEN'. Migrants then had to sleep in the streets and parks of the town, particularly the Parc Saint-Pierre, opposite the town hall.

La Belle Étoile and the other organizations grouped in the C'SUR (Collectif de Soutien d'Urgence aux Refoulés [Emergency Migrant Support Collective])[1] immediately challenged the authorities on the basis of discussions on the accommodation of migrants that had already been started. A hangar was opened for them on 24 April, with tents inside for sleeping, sanitary facilities, and prefabs for administration and meals. Management of this was handed to La Belle Étoile. It was only open at night, from 6 pm to 9 am. Initially envisaged to accommodate eighty, it would soon house between 120 and 200, varying from night to night.

On 1 June 1999, the prefect announced that the hangar would close on 4 June. The migrants then once again found

themselves sleeping in former blockhouses, abandoned buildings, and parks. The Parc Saint-Pierre became a shantytown.
Having tried other means of pressure, the sub-prefect ordered
voluntary organizations to stop all assistance, under threat
of legal action.

The stand-off between the organizations and the state
continued, and following a visit from the prefect to Pas-de-
Calais, the interior ministry decided to open three sites of
temporary accommodation: an outbuilding of the hospital for
families, a holiday centre for individuals in an illegal situation
and awaiting expulsion, and a hangar that was used in the
construction of the Channel Tunnel for single women and
men – located at Sangatte, a commune adjacent to Calais.

This arrangement, opened in a number of stages during the
month of August, closed on 31 August 1999. Then there was
a return to the blockhouses, public parks, abandoned buildings and waste ground. A new balance of forces came into
being between the voluntary organizations and the state. At
the beginning of September, the organizations, along with a
hundred migrants, tried to reopen the hangar in Calais that
had been opened and then closed some months earlier. The
attempt failed, and those involved went on to demonstrate at
the sub-prefecture. With the threat of a visit from Abbé Pierre
the following week, the state gave in and agreed to reopen the
Sangatte hangar, which it did on 24 September 1999.

1999–2000: the Sangatte moment

In the shadow of the Sangatte centre, border control measures
were strengthened; this would lead to a greater dispersal of
migrants, right along the coastline from Brittany to Belgium,
and along the motorways leading to Calais, close to the
parking areas for lorries heading to the UK. Hiding in a lorry
that would cross the Channel by ferry, or on the rail shuttles
that used the Tunnel, became the main technique for crossing the border.

Controls on the British side had already been strengthened
over the last few years. This process was completed with the
Immigration and Asylum Act of 1999, which would subtly
reinforce the control of vehicles at French ports. The British

authorities decided to impose on carriers a fine of £2,000 for each person found hidden in a vehicle. The multiplication of checks before embarkation increased the time spent on boarding the ferries, which slowed economic activity and made the port less competitive. At Calais, the management of the port turned logic upside down, claiming that the controls made it possible for transporters to avoid fines, and facilitated the smooth course of economic activity. The Chambres de Commerce et d'Industrie, which manage the Channel and North Sea ports, would accordingly extend these controls in the coming years.

In 2000, the port of Calais was surrounded by a fence 2.80 metres high, equipped with a detection system, which cut it off from the urban space. Video surveillance cameras were installed, and CO_2 gas detectors were used to detect human presence within lorries.

Crossing attempts, which had been made chiefly through the port, now switched to the Tunnel. In the course of 2001, the fences surrounding the site were doubled and topped with razor wire, the site was equipped with surveillance cameras, and trees and bushes were cut down to improve visibility. In 2002, new fences surrounded the area where lorries were loaded onto the rail shuttles, and the British army loaned a Passive Millimetric Wave Imager to scan lorries.

These difficulties increased the time spent at Calais before crossing the border, which partly explains the increase in the number of migrants present. But other ports and occasional crossing sites also became places of constant transit, where encampments and squats appeared. Other ports then also equipped themselves with control arrangements, such as Dieppe in 2001 and Cherbourg in 2002 (fences, cameras, thermal and CO_2 detectors).

Bound up with the strengthening of controls, there was increasing evidence of police violence in the context of arrests, without this phenomenon yet becoming commonplace as it would be in the following years.

On 26 September 2002, at a trilateral meeting in Zeebrugge, the Belgian, British and French interior ministers agreed to establish common immigration controls. They saw 'the actions that they had decided ... as an essential step in the establishment of an integrated management of the external borders of the European Union'.[2] For European officials, this border became a model to follow in terms of management. The British controls were extended to ports in Belgium (Ostend and Zeebrugge), then to the Netherlands in 2003–4.

2002: British control at the port of Calais

The decision to close the Sangatte centre was made on 12 July 2002. According to the French government, the reason was 'to send the whole world a signal, to say that it is no longer worth coming to this hangar at the end of the world, as there is no future for [migrants] in these conditions'.[3]

The UN High Commissioner for Refugees (UNHCR) supported the French and British authorities in this operation. It carried out an information campaign about asylum among refugees, and was charged with registering people accommodated in the Red Cross centre at Sangatte. This step particularly enabled specific cases of so-called vulnerable persons to be noted (unaccompanied minors, some of whom had families in England, single women, the sick and the injured, etc.), which would then be dealt with by the UN agency.

Based on a tripartite plan signed by the Afghan government shortly before, the French government and the UNHCR offered Afghan refugees a voluntary return plan, with financial compensation of €2,000 per person (and an additional €500 per child). Only eleven people agreed to be repatriated to Afghanistan.

Ultimately, of the 1,268 foreigners who received support in leaving the Sangatte camp when it was closed, eleven agreed to return to Afghanistan, thirty-five were (re)admitted to other European countries, and 1,032 were transferred to the UK. The British authorities undertook to take the greater part of the foreigners in the Sangatte camp, including almost the total number of Iraqis (893).

After 5 November 2002, access to the Sangatte centre was no longer possible for refugees who had not been able to register, or for new arrivals. Police were now posted at the entrance, banning access to all persons who had not received badges given out at the count carried out by the UNHCR. To challenge this rejection, refugees, helped by activists and volunteers from the organizations, occupied several public and private buildings, particularly places of worship. Faced with this mobilization, the prefecture eventually gave in and agreed that those refugees whose badges had been de-activated could re-enter the centre, the others remaining excluded.

The start of December 2002 marked the definitive end point of any possibilities of accommodation in the Sangatte centre. The camp was officially closed on 31 December, and the former Channel Tunnel hangar demolished a few days later.

The long years of eviction

The closing of the Sangatte centre opened a new phase in the process of externalizing UK border controls onto French soil. This was expressed in December 2002 by the establishment of the police operations known as Concorde and Ulysse, which mobilized six companies of the CRS (Compagnies Républicaines de Sécurité) along with two police squadrons with the aim of 'managing the problems of public order arising from the closure of the centre, as well as the removal of migrants from the Calais area'.[4]

The Ulysse police operation would be repeated several times in the period that followed the closing of the Sangatte centre. Its main aim was to remove the refugees from the Calais area by way of mass arrests, the refugees then being expelled from French territory or else dispersed across the region. This system included in particular a mechanism of tight control when the refugee benefited from an offer of temporary accommodation. Deprived of the possibility of applying for asylum, if refugees refused or hesitated to demand assistance for voluntary return, they would then be almost immediately issued with an order of expulsion from France. In December 2006, this procedure was applied to refugees as they came out of their temporary accommodation, and they were directly placed in a detention centre.

This logic of harassment and dissuasion was also expressed in the opening on 2 January 2003 of a detention centre at Coquelles, a commune adjacent to Calais. Refugees issued with expulsion orders risked being detained here if they were stopped in the streets of Calais, even if they had come from a country at war to which it was practically impossible to return them. The migrants affected by the 'Dublin regulations' likewise risked expulsion, though this was not always effective. They might then be released and find themselves again wandering around, before being stopped again and possibly again detained. Ultimately, the 'detention' option would be added to the long list of police dissuasion tactics applied in the post-Sangatte phase.

On 4 February 2003, the French and British authorities signed a new bilateral agreement, the Le Touquet treaty. Negotiated in the wake of the closing of the Red Cross camp at Sangatte, this context weighed heavily on the content of the text. The agreement provided for the possibility of bilateral border controls at all the sea ports on the Channel and North Sea, a new step in the logic of externalization of the UK border. In contrast to previous agreements, the measures adopted were dependent on financial and material assistance from Britain. In the end, the Le Touquet treaty generalized the gradual implementation during 2003 of a system that imposed financial penalties on transporters if a refugee was discovered under a lorry or within a trailer (£2,000 per person discovered).

In the immediate post-Sangatte phase, refugees obliged to flee from police harassment found refuge in the town wherever they could. They sheltered in blockhouses, which were walled up after the police discovered them, settled in abandoned buildings, or put together rudimentary shelters in wooded spaces, using tarpaulins and pallets.

Geographically, after initially remaining around the centre of Sangatte, the migrants moved towards Calais town, and particularly the industrial zone of Les Dunes, where the Tioxide plant is located, and the woods of Dubrulle and Les Garennes. Successive squats and encampments were established here until 2015.

The closing of the Sangatte centre increased the dispersal of refugees to other crossing points. Inland from Calais, at Norrent-Fontes, Angres and Steenvoorde, new staging-posts appeared on the migration routes, whose names would become part of the migrants' mental geography (see map 2). Further south, Paris became the place that refugees headed

The 'Jungles'

ZEEBRUGGE
DUNKIRK
LOON-PLAGE
CALAIS
GRANDE-SYNTHE
STEENVOORDE
TATINGHEM
NORRENT-FONTES
ANGRES

United Kingdom

English Channel

N

DIEPPE

OUISTREHAM

CHERBOURG

SAINT-MALO

ROSCOFF

France

PARIS (METRO STALINGRAD)

50 km

● 'Migrant camps'**

⦂ 'Organized inhospitality'***

↝ Crossing points to the UK
(by boat or train)

(*) Self-constructed, precarious and temporary camps, abandoned buildings, ruins, etc.

(**) Since the evacuation of the Calais Jungle and the burning of the Grande-Synthe humanitarian camp, the police have been pursuing a policy of daily harassment against exiles, preventing the setting up of 'safe havens'. This situation is also found in Paris and Steenvoorde, although police harassment is somewhat less oppressive there.

Map designed by Nicolas LAMBERT & Maël GALISSON, 2017

Map 2. Jungles, encampments and localities mentioned.

for, or fell back to when police pressure at Calais became too strong. Thus, in Paris, just after the closing of the Red Cross camp at Sangatte, they settled in the Square Alban-Satragne, as observed by activists of the collective Exilés du 10e Arrondissement, which was formed at that point.[5] Over time, and as expulsions took place, other public spaces were used as refuges and occupied by migrants, from the Square Vuillemin to the area below the overhead Métro at La Chapelle.

2009: 'The closing of the Calais Jungle': a new media sequence

The aggravation of the conflict in Afghanistan after 2005 led to the arrival of a larger number of Afghan refugees in Europe, which became a sensitive issue at the UK border. In autumn 2008, Afghan refugees at Calais were the object of raids followed up by detention. Joint Franco–British flights were projected, to organize expulsions to Afghanistan. This situation aroused a strong mobilization on the part of voluntary organizations, and the European Court of Human Rights suspended these expulsions.

The situation of migrants along the coast had meanwhile become more visible, with an increase in their number and the publication of the report of the Coordination Française pour le Droit d'Asile (CFDA) in September 2008, entitled 'La Loi des Jungles'.

The government then constructed a sequence of media events in 2009, focusing on visits to Calais by the minister for immigration and national identity, Éric Besson. On 27 January, he arrived to 'acquaint himself with the situation', promised to 'make the border watertight', and committed himself to return before 1 May to 'present solutions' to the situation. He returned on 23 April and presented a plan in two parts. The first part, under the heading 'firmness', provided for the 'closing' of squats and encampments before the end of the year. The second, headed 'humanity', took up a certain number of points discussed between the voluntary organizations and the town hall: the creation of a site for distributing meals, a day centre and a place for showers (this part would be financed by local authorities, and operated by the voluntary organizations on an unpaid basis). Added to these were the opening of an office for registering asylum requests at the Calais sub-prefecture, and an office for assistance with voluntary returns. On 21 April, a raid was carried out in the Afghans' encampment, with the arrest of 200 people, who were taken into custody but later released. The operation was presented as a 'rehearsal' for the demolition of what was then called the 'Calais Jungle'.

Subsequent to the opening of the office for registering asylum requests, the UNHCR opened an office of its own in Calais to give information about asylum, jointly with France Terre d'Asile. The majority of the voluntary organizations in the Calais region gradually began to assist asylum seekers with their applications.

The number of migrants in Calais continued to increase, reaching a figure of 1,200 to 1,400 by July 2009. It then rapidly declined, as the border crossing suddenly became easier in the course of the summer. But this fall was also bound up, on the one hand, with the agreements between Libya and Italy that made the Mediterranean crossing more difficult, and on the other, with a large proportion of the Afghans heading instead towards Scandinavia.

The destruction of the Calais encampments in autumn 2009 was preceded by the evacuation in August of those around the Gare de l'Est in Paris, as well as the destruction of the Patras shantytown in Greece in early July. This had existed for twelve years, and its destruction marked a reorientation of transit routes to the port of Igoumenitsa, and to the land route across the Balkans.[6]

The destruction of the encampments took place between 22 September and 7 October 2009. It began with the 'closing' of the 'Jungle de Calais', a shantytown located on waste ground in one of the town's industrial zones (see photo 1). The operation was announced in advance by the minister for immigration, who visited there on the first afternoon, following its evacuation and during its destruction, and was widely publicized. This encampment, which originated in 2008 amid operations of destruction that had led migrants to move from one place to another in the zone, had grown to 900 people in July 2009, then fallen back to 600 occupants

Photo 1. The 'Calais Jungle', also known as the 'Pashtun Jungle', destroyed in September 2009 (photo: Sara Prestianni, July 2009).

by early September, but half of these had left the site after
the announcement of its pending evacuation and before this
was carried out. Finally, 278 individuals were arrested, and
individuals categorized 'by appearance' as either adults or
minors. Minors were taken to centres opened for the occasion, with the majority leaving these in the following days.
The adults, or those considered so by the police, were sent
to detention centres throughout France, from which almost
all were released by local judges in view of the irregular
character of the proceedings. Only nine people arrested on
22 September and the following days, who had not lodged
an appeal after arriving in the detention centre, were actually
expelled to Afghanistan, on a charter flight organized jointly
with the UK. The interior minister returned to Calais on 2
October. To mark his visit, the Sudanese encampment had
been evacuated that morning, and the Eritreans' squat was
demolished at lunchtime. Around 600 migrants were present
at Calais before the start of the expulsions. By the month of
November, their number had stabilized at around 400.

Several days before the evacuation of 22 September 2009,
an organized national presentation in the press and on TV
prepared people for the event, designed as a symbol of the
expulsion of foreigners and protection of French territory:
words and images were widely circulated to show a marginal
and frightening world, 'organized crime', 'mafias' of people-
smugglers, horrific destitution.

The network of voluntary organizations

The first form of solidarity to develop was that of neighbours.
With the increase in the number of migrants blocked on
the Channel coast during the 1990s, women and men who
offered informal help, a hot meal, sometimes accommodation, gradually organized themselves into more formal structures. La Belle Étoile, the first formal organization officially
created under the prevailing legislation, was founded in 1994,
with the objective of 'informing, advising, freely assisting
morally and legally...any passing foreigner in difficulty in
the Calais region'.

Individual solidarity did not always depend on organized
bodies. To give someone a hot meal, to recharge their mobile

phone, to put them up, to help them financially, were often isolated actions of individuals from communities more or less close to the encampments or crossing points. In a context of repression for the 'offence of solidarity', these people organized themselves into collectives. The Collectif de Soutien d'Urgence aux Refoulés (C'SUR) was formed during winter 1997 with the aim of facilitating the organization of material and political support to Roma refugees from the Czech Republic who were not admitted to the UK. It was then made up of La Belle Étoile, local groups of the Salvation Army, the Comité Catholique Contre la Faim et Pour le Développement, as well as the Calais section of the Ligue des Droits de l'Homme and the Association d'Entraide du Calaisis. Later on, this collective would be joined by other organizations (the Scouts et Guides de France, Secours Catholique, the local section of Les Verts, Salam), and it changed its name to Collectif de Soutien d'Urgence aux Réfugiés. The collective began to break up with the departure of Salam and Secours Catholique, and eventually it was dissolved. The Salam association, founded in 2003, came out of this collective, with the aim of providing humanitarian assistance to migrants, as well as supporting volunteers who were prosecuted for actions of solidarity. The Auberge des Migrants was formed in 2008 by a core of volunteers from other organizations, in the context of sharp tensions with the public authorities and divisions over the position to adopt. (The member associations of C'SUR had decided on a 'strike', to force the state to intervene on behalf of the migrants, while Salam, which had left this collective, continued its activities.) The appearance of encampments inland from Calais, as well as at the other Channel ports, led to the creation of activist organizations or collectives with the missions of assisting and supporting the refugees living in these shantytowns. Thus, organizations such as Itinérance arose at Cherbourg in 2008, and Terre d'Errance at Norrent-Fontes in 2008. The year 2009 saw the creation of Terre d'Errance at Steenvoorde, as well as the collective Fraternité Migrants Bassin Minier 62 at Angres, to give only a few examples.

In 2008, the Coordination Française Pour le Droit d'Asile conducted a major study of the whole of the northern coastline, meeting with a number of voluntary organizations and activists. This investigative work led to the publication of a report, 'La Loi des Jungles', and served as a basis for networking several organizations and activists involved locally in support for refugees. This dynamic was expressed the following year by the establishment of the informal 'Jungles' network, a mailing list that also held meetings between the voluntary organizations, enabling different participants to exchange information and get to know one another. In 2011 it was decided to give this network a firmer structure, and it formalized its statutes as an association (under the law of 1901) under the name Plateforme de Services aux Migrants, with the aim of 'sharing experiences, resources and skills to organize a better defence of the rights of refugees'.

At Norrent-Fontes, a small commune some 75 kilometres south of Calais, there have been encampments of migrants since 2006–7 (see photo 2). Despite these being regularly destroyed by the police, refugees in transit continued to return to the region, on account of a parking area for lorries close by. At the municipal elections of March 2008, Marc Boulnois, a member of Europe-Écologie/Les Verts, was elected mayor. A new phase opened under his mandate, breaking with the logic of expulsions. The mayor agreed that refugees could now establish themselves on a strip alongside a municipal footpath between two agricultural holdings. Their situation here was still precarious, but they no longer had to fear forced evacuation.[7]

Photo 2. The Norrent-Fontes encampment, 2016 (photo: Julien Saison).

However, the state agencies remained set on a policy of dissuasion by expulsion. In 2010, a stand-off began between the state and the municipality of Norrent-Fontes. On two occasions (December 2010 and November 2011) the state ordered the town hall to demolish the camp, which it refused to do. This situation mobilized a number of people, including members of the municipal council, who organized themselves informally. Outside the commune, a network of support for the mayor of Norrent-Fontes was formed in the region, the Réseau des Élus Hospitaliers, its members including the mayor of Grand-Synthe, Damien Carême (Parti Socialiste), the mayor of Angres, Maryse Roger-Coupin (Parti Communiste Français) and Hélène Flautre, a European deputy (Europe-Écologies/Les Verts).

Initially a network of vigilance born as a reaction to attacks from the state, this group structured itself into a formal organization with the mission of 'supporting elected local officials acting in conformity with human rights … particularly those who receive migrants and ensure them access to basic services, and more broadly persons in difficulty on their territory, as much as their means allow, with the assistance and support of voluntary organizations and local residents.'[8] In the face of national migration policies that were hostile to the refugees, this network sought to promote an alternative reception policy.

At Norrent-Fontes, Angres and Grande-Synthe, mayors attempted to put this vision into practice. There was dialogue and sometimes even real cooperation with voluntary organizations locally involved in seeking to improve conditions of life for the migrants. At Norrent-Fontes, groups of huts were erected, and the mayor regularly distributed a tank of water; at Angres, the town hall tolerated the squatting of a municipal building by the refugees; at Grand-Synthe, tents and then huts were constructed, and the town hall loaned a heating system for the winter period.

A brief ray of light

The results of the presidential and legislative elections of May and June 2012 did not lead to changes in the ways in which the state and its services operated. In September 2012, at Calais, there were several expulsions of squats and encampments of refugees: individuals were arrested by the police, some were placed in a detention centre and their personal effects destroyed or confiscated. No alternative accommodation was offered, and the migrants were left without shelter.

However, it was in this context that the prefect of Pas-de-Calais decided to establish a 'round table on the situation of migrant populations in Pas-de-Calais'.[9] Drawing on the circular of 26 August 2012,[10] he invited some of the voluntary organizations to 'study together solutions that might improve the situation and enable each party to carry out its mission with respect for the law'. Between October 2012 and December 2013, these meetings remained quite formal and did not give rise to any significant advance. And yet this 'consultation body' at least enabled the organizations to renew a dialogue with the administration that had not existed since 2009.

At Calais in December 2013, Manuel Valls, then interior minister, chaired one of these meetings in the context of this consultation body. Despite having announced new reinforcements the same morning on a visit to the local police, in the afternoon he promised the voluntary organizations the experiment of a 'Maison des Migrants', a reception facility conceived and supported by some of their number. With the director of social cohesion for the Pas-de-Calais department as intermediary, the interior minister explained this measure, which aimed to 'consider the establishment of reception structures reserved for migrants, where these persons can stay, look after themselves and reflect on their project, to decide whether they wish to go to England, remain in France, or return to their country of origin'.[11] In this perspective, the state services envisaged a diagnosis, in consultation with the voluntary organizations, of the state of migrant encampments in the north of France.

In November 2013, in parallel with these discussions, came the legal decision to close a squat on the Rue Victor Hugo in Calais. This uninhabited building had been opened and occupied by No Border activists to create accommodation for the so-called vulnerable category of refugees (women, children, sick and injured men). An expulsion procedure had been initiated by the proprietor, and led to an expulsion notice.

The prefect of Pas-de-Calais then declared that there would be no expulsion without a rehousing solution. A phase of discussion and negotiation began between the state services, the voluntary organizations, and the No Border activists: in the end, the association Solid'R, which operated in the field of social action, was commissioned by the state to take over management of the building. Social workers gave the squat's inhabitants support before these moved into another building, leaving the original one at the disposal of its owner. The new site, known by the social workers assigned there as '*la maison des femmes*', was the successful version of a reception site for refugees in transit.

This relatively favourable political context did not last. After the European and municipal elections of spring 2014, marked by a serious reversal for the left in power, government positions hardened. The state no longer continued with the project of establishing 'Maisons des Migrants' on French territory. On the contrary, its first decisions for Calais after the election were expressed on 21 May 2014 in the expulsion of migrants from several encampments, without either consultation or a rehousing solution. On the pretext of a sanitary operation of treatment against scabies, the inhabitants of three encampments were evacuated and left destitute. At large in the Calais town centre, the refugees ended up congregating around a site close to the port where meals were distributed, which had been put at the disposal of the voluntary organizations for the purpose of food distribution. This site was first and foremost a refuge for nearly 500 migrants with no other shelter. It served as a living space where several communities and nationalities coexisted, not without difficulty, and also became a site of political action. After several days here, some twenty individuals decided to begin a hunger strike to defend their rights and have their situation regularized.

Faced with this situation, the state stuck to its positions and could only propose the regular asylum procedure, accommodation arrangements for which were already saturated, due to a lack of places or the risk for certain refugees of expulsion to another European country if that was where their arrival in Europe was first recorded (according to the terms of the 'Dublin III' regulations). Moreover, an order against the distribution site was initiated by the Calais town hall on

24 June 2014. The evacuation took place in the morning of 2 July, with the backing of a substantial police presence. It also affected three squatted buildings that had been opened up by No Border activists, in which asylum seekers who had not been offered accommodation found refuge. All witnesses, whether activists, representatives of the voluntary organizations or journalists, were hastily pushed away.

A sorting was conducted at the distribution site, lasting throughout the day. Buses were stationed close to the area, and left Calais one by one. Women and children were sent to centres without the organizations managing these centres being informed in advance. More than 200 men were placed in detention centres, from which the majority were released on grounds of breaches of legal procedure. Some of the buses drove for dozens of kilometres, then stopped and abandoned their passengers in the middle of nowhere. The asylum seekers dislodged from squats in the town centre were left in the street. In the end, only a few days after this 'scattering' operation, which was marked by violence and improvisation, several hundred migrants returned to Calais, having fled from the unsuitable accommodation offered or after their release from detention centres.

In response to this operation, voluntary organizations and activists organized a demonstration on 12 July 2014, attended by some 500 people, that concluded with the opening of a squat on the site of a disused factory building of the Galoo company.

The rise of the far right

Hostility to the presence of refugees in the Calais region dates back several years. During the 'Sangatte moment', the expression of xenophobia had in particular taken the form of an unsigned leaflet titled 'Bienvenue à Croix-Rouge Center Parcs' [Welcome to Red Cross Center Parcs], its sarcastic tone denouncing the fact that migrants supposedly benefited 'without charge for goods and services paid for by local taxpayers', and concluding: 'At your Red Cross Center Parcs, you will find staff available to organize your travel abroad!'

The No Border activists, who had been present at Calais since summer 2009 and were supported by antifascist activists from the region, then stepped up their work of monitoring violence against the refugees. They thus noted several acts of aggression, one of which was perpetrated in autumn 2010 by a group of far-right activists towards several Sudanese refugees. The aggressors, close to skinhead movements, were in due course given prison sentences.[12] In most cases, however, those guilty of such acts are not discovered, either because the refugees who are their victims do not choose to make a complaint, or because the inquiry is inconclusive.

On top of these acts of violence, the migrants faced discriminatory practices on a daily basis. A number of managers of cafés and shops banned migrants (and sometimes also their supporters) from entering their premises, on the pretext that it would cause them to lose customers. When a squat opened, neighbours sometimes protested against the occupation by starting a petition. However, the majority of the Calais population remained indifferent to the presence of refugees on the margins of their town.

From 2013, however, hostility to foreigners in Calais would take a more structured form and occupy a greater place in public debate, encouraged by certain positions adopted by the mayor of the town, Natacha Bouchart, a member of Les Républicains. On 23 October 2013, she posted on her Facebook page a message inviting the inhabitants of Calais to denounce any squat that they were aware of, or any attempt at such. A few weeks earlier, she had declared to the press, speaking of the 'migrant problem', that the town of Calais had been 'taken hostage'.[13]

Two days later, a Calais resident responded positively to the call launched by Natacha Bouchart, and started a Facebook page headed 'Sauvons Calais' [Save Calais]. This informal group presented itself as non-political, and took as its mission to 'struggle against immigration, pro-migrant associations and foreigner preference'.[14] Seeing itself as representing the dissatisfaction of Calais locals, it demanded 'the expulsion of migrants from Calais territory', 'the arrest of any person sheltering illegals', as well as 'the banning of the Salam association and the "No Border" movement'.[15]

Rapidly, and profiting from the growing audience on social networks, members of 'Sauvons Calais' decided to take to the streets. On 7 November 2013, several dozen people responded to a call to gather in front of the town hall, with banners 'Stop mass immigration to Calais' or simply 'Fed Up!' One of the deputy mayors came out to greet the demonstrators and discuss with them. On 11 January 2014, the group organized a second street action, demonstrating with slogans such as 'Calais for its own people' and 'This is our home'. Some fifty people took part in the demonstration.

In mid-February 2014, housing rights activists occupied an abandoned smallholding at Coulogne, a commune bordering on Calais. Their objective was to show that there are places in and around Calais where it is possible to accommodate homeless people. Very soon notified of this, supporters of 'Sauvons Calais' used their Facebook page to call for people to demonstrate around the smallholding. At first they were scarcely a dozen, but some days later seventy people turned up to denounce the existence of this squat. The demonstrators organized night-time patrols, and kept up a daily presence. On several occasions, and sometimes under the eyes of the CRS, the squat became the target of projectiles (stones, Molotov cocktails), as well as an attempt by two participants to break into the premises. Faced with the dangers around them, the housing rights activists ultimately abandoned the occupation scarcely a week after it had begun.

In this way 'Sauvons Calais' gained visibility. The discourse of the group steadily radicalized, and the masks fell away. Its ties with the Front National and other far-right groups were revealed. A photo of the leader of 'Sauvons Calais' circulated on social media, proudly displaying a swastika tattooed on his chest. The activists supporting the refugees were the target of physical aggression. The group gradually attracted other far-right groups around it (from the Parti de la France, founded by dissidents from the Front National, the legally dissolved movement L'Œuvre Française, and the Identités network which is close to the Bloc Identitaire). At a meeting in September 2014, in front of a banner demanding 'Throw Them Out', a leader called on an audience of some 300 persons, including a group of skinheads with 'SS' tattoos or dressed in T-shirts celebrating the Charlemagne division, to:[16] 'Come together, organize by district, don't let them get away with it! Don't let them throttle you! Defend yourselves, legitimate defence!'[17] Then, in October 2014, the police union SGP-FO organized a demonstration to protest against the 'continual flow of migrants, which is bringing the local economy into unprecedented crisis and threatening businesses'.[18] Some 300 persons participated in this mobilization, including police, farmers and shopkeepers, behind a banner 'Support the Police'. Bit by bit, the self-fulfilling prophecy of the mayor of Calais, Natacha Bouchart, was realized. By dint of repeating throughout the interview that 'the people of Calais have had enough', the latter began to genuinely believe this. New actors (shopkeepers, management and unions at the port), who had previously been rather discreet, now took a position on 'the subject of migrants'. On top of this, the appearance on the Calais political scene of an openly xenophobic group in the form of 'Sauvons Calais' placed the mayor in the position of a responsible actor, competent to handle the situation.

The clearly proclaimed position of 'Sauvons Calais' on the far-right fringe did the group a disservice and confined it to a politically limited audience. In autumn 2015, the group celebrated two years of existence by organizing a public meeting, but which attracted only a few people. However, its emergence served as a trigger for several other initiatives. Between November 2015 and February 2016, the French branch of the Islamophobic movement Pegida established itself and organized demonstrations. In parallel with this, several Facebook pages were created by individuals who presented themselves as apolitical and simply as 'spokespeople' for the discontent of the Calais inhabitants. At the end of 2015, when the Jungle had been in existence for several months, a new group was created, 'Calaisiens en Colère' [angry Calaisians], which organized patrols in support of residents living close to the Jungle, and assisted the CRS with their interventions. On 17 December 2015, they organized a demonstration of support for neighbours of the Jungle, which was joined by members of another far-right splinter group – the Mouvement d'Action Sociale, close to the Greek neo-Nazis of the Golden Dawn and the Italian neo-fascists of Casa Pound. At the same time, Facebook pages of 'Calais libre' and 'Reprenons Calais' appeared with a similar discourse, before being removed by the social network for stirring up hatred.

The number of violent and racist acts towards the refugees increased. During the night of 20–21 January 2016, three migrants of Syrian nationality were attacked by six men who disguised themselves as police and were armed with telescopic truncheons. In the night of 10–11 February 2016, at Loon-Plage near Dunkirk, four refugees of Kurdish origin were attacked by seven men, several of whom came from Calais, and whom the police report recognized as 'having come to Loon-Plage to exercise violence against migrants with blunt instruments'.[19]

September 2014 onward: concentrate, disperse, control

The number of refugees on the UK border increased again from summer 2013, and by summer 2014 there was a spread of encampments at the ports from Brittany to Belgium, as well as on the motorways leading to these and by service stations in the Nord-Pas-de-Calais region, Picardy and Belgium.

This new situation led to a series of new Franco–British agreements, in 2014, 2015 and 2016, which resumed and amplified the repressive measures contained in the agreement of 2009, adding a calculated financial contribution from the UK side, 'humanitarian measures' (including assistance to return), and joint initiatives in the EU institutions to strengthen controls of the external EU border.

The way that the state handled this situation differed from place to place. At Calais, the congregation of the migrant population on a single site (in April 2015) led to a complex pattern combining an official camp (with containers) and a shantytown. In the Dunkirk region (Grande-Synthe) and in Paris, camps were set up by the municipality, and only subsequently did the state get involved and take control of the initiative. This policy of local congregation was accompanied by a subsequent dispersal across the whole country, by way of the Centres d'Accueil et d'Orientation. Elsewhere, in the smaller encampments, the policy of eviction, begun with the closing of the Sangatte centre in 2002, was continued (Chocques, Dieppe, Cherbourg, Caen, Steenvoorde, Norrent-Fontes, etc.).

Calais

At Calais, in September 2016 more than 10,000 people were living on a complex site that contained both the shantytown and structures erected by the state – the Jules Ferry centre with a platform of daytime services and accommodation for women and children with 400 places, and a container camp with 1,500 places. This was the result of the desire of the authorities to concentrate the migrants present in the Calais region on a single site, so as to remove them from the town and control them better.[20] Some of the humanitarian organizations had participated both in the transfer of people to this site up to its subsequent evacuation, in a form of joint management with the state that was sometimes conflictual.

State policy grows less flexible

As we have seen above, the brutal resumption of expulsions from the encampments on 28 May 2014 led to a response from the migrants, who occupied the site arranged for the distribution of meals, evacuated on 2 July of the same year. Here, it was the voluntary organizations that mobilized, opening a large squat in the town centre at the end of a demonstration.

It is probable that this was the moment when representatives of the state began to wonder how they might obtain the consent of the organizations. They had also to find a response to the already substantial rise in the number of migrants present at Calais. One demand of the organizations was for a secure site from which the migrants would no longer be expelled, as a basis for an improvement in their living conditions. The Calais town hall, for its part, wanted them to disappear from the town centre. A compromise was thus found to resettle the migrants close to the premises of a leisure centre, where various services could be brought together and financed (showers, meals, access to health care and information), as well as accommodation for women and children. Though expulsion only required the police, the participation of the organizations was necessary to gather the migrants together in one place. Their consent was obtained by telling them that migrants would be 'tolerated' on this site, which the organizations interpreted as meaning 'will not be expelled'.

A policy of removal

The departure of migrants from the centre of Calais was a political decision on the part of the mayor, who was already conducting an active policy of relocation. This was expressed in the refusal of bookings of municipal premises for activities of solidarity with the migrants, a call for people to inform the authorities about squats, a decree prohibiting the holding of an intercultural festival, a ban on access to municipal football grounds in autumn 2013, and a change in the regulations of the médiathèque (autumn 2014), then those of a swimming pool (spring 2015), so that access for migrants was de facto prohibited.

Even before the transfer of migrants in spring 2015, a proliferation of far-right groups calling themselves 'anti-migrant', and demonstrations by local people and police, had prepared minds for the removal, which then seemed an obvious decision.

From shantytown to shantytown camp

The site where the migrants were taken by the voluntary associations in April 2015 was partly a former dump for building rubble and partly a sandy area, some of which was covered with thorny bushes and another part marshy. The only water supply was at the entrance to the Jules Ferry centre, several hundred metres away. The closest shop was three-quarters of an hour's walk. Some 1,500 people settled here between late March and early April 2015.

The municipality rapidly erected an earthwork barrier east of the shantytown that was taking shape, along the road leading to the Jules Ferry centre, to reassure local residents. A few weeks later, the state erected a double barrier topped by barbed wire to the west, alongside the ring road leading to the port. The migrants had in fact been settled close to one of the main crossing points to the UK.

The installation of the refugees was assisted to a large degree by the voluntary organizations, something that had never been known at the other sites that had previously existed. As well as cabins, a church and mosques were constructed, also schools and other collective facilities. Shops sprung up very rapidly, followed by restaurants. These had already existed in some of the preceding encampments, those furthest from the town, but here the isolation and the growth in population led to their rapid proliferation.

The rising population of the shantytown, however, soon outstripped the capacities of the voluntary organizations – the services proposed by La Vie Active, which had been commissioned by the state to manage the Jules Ferry centre, being insufficient right from the start. National NGOs began to intervene in the summer of 2015. The wide media coverage of what was called the 'migrant crisis', and the hostile attitude of European governments, led to the arrival of a number of volunteers, mainly British, but also from other European countries. These gradually developed a range of activities. Humanitarian assistance was supplemented by the creation of new collective facilities in the shantytown (schools, library, theatre, centres for women and children, for young people, radio, etc.).

With the evacuation of the last remaining encampments in the centre of Calais, at the end of September 2015, the authorities steadily increased the visible police presence around the shantytown, replacing the policy of expulsion from one site to another, which had been applied since the closing of the Sangatte centre, with a policy of expulsion 'on the spot' by the destruction of parts of the shantytown. These periodic destructions expressed a policy of control and pressure designed to contain the number of inhabitants. At the end of September 2015, they affected a part of the shantytown that was expanding beneath the ring road to the port, then in November the area where a container camp financed by the state would be constructed, in January a 100-metre band along the ring road and an adjacent road, and in March the entire southern half of the shantytown.

In November 2015, the state was legally constrained to provide a minimum in the way of improvements to render the living conditions less undignified. It commissioned an international NGO, ACTED, to undertake these works. But ACTED also acquired the role of coordinating the different voluntary actors and running a council of community representatives to interface with the prefecture and the police. Starting in May 2016, the prefecture banned the bringing of construction material onto the site, all entries to which were controlled by the police, forcing the organizations to negotiate each time they wanted to undertake a new construction. Within a few months, a shantytown built by its inhabitants and voluntary organizations had developed into a composite site made up of three elements. First, there was the Jules Ferry centre, a service platform in the daytime and with overnight accommodation for 400 women and children. Then there was the container camp with 1,500 places. Both of these were financed by the state and run by a voluntary organization that this commissioned. Finally, a shantytown where a form of joint management with the state was practised, coordinated by another organization that it commissioned, while at the same time a relatively autonomous social, urban and cultural life developed, as we shall see in the following chapters.

Around Dunkirk

Around Dunkirk there were several small encampments, each generally housing a few dozen migrants: at Loon-Plage close to the ferry port, and at Grande-Synthe and Téteghem near motorway service stations. When the one at Téteghem was closed, the migrants went by car to rest stops in Belgium, or climbed into the lorries that stopped close by on the motorway, with the connivance of the driver.

The Loon-Plage encampment was destroyed on several occasions. The Grande-Synthe encampment was established on land belonging to the municipality, and the one at Téteghem on land belonging to the Dunkirk urban district. In spring 2012, huts were erected, and basic facilities installed to improve living conditions somewhat.

In November 2014, given the increasing number of persons in the encampment, the Téteghem town hall erected a container camp of eighty places, with the declared aim of setting a limit to the number of persons on the site. The former encampment was destroyed. But this did not prevent small camps being established around the container camp, and the number of people there continued to rise, reaching several hundred by autumn 2015. The container camp was dismantled on 18 November, and the encampments around it demolished.

The encampment at Grande-Synthe, which housed some eighty occupants in early summer 2015, underwent a very rapid growth later in the summer and into the autumn, reaching more than 2,500 by the month of November. The town hall, which had envisaged installing heated tents for the winter, then containers to accommodate the growing number of people there, was rapidly overtaken by events. Material conditions soon deteriorated on this very muddy site, all the more so as the police blocked the entry of tents and materials for the construction of huts.

Médecins Sans Frontières (MSF) then proposed establishing a refugee camp on another site offered by the municipality, to international standards and with 2,500 places. Despite opposition from the state, this camp opened at the beginning of March 2016. The number of migrants actually fell, and only 1,500 moved there.

Three months later, on 30 May 2016, the interior minister, accompanied by the housing minister, visited Grande-Synthe and announced that the state would take over the running of the camp. The organization managing it was changed, Utopia 56 being replaced by the Association Flandres Enfance Jeunesse Insertion (AFEJI), whose president had been mayor of Dunkirk for twenty-five years, and several times a minister in the Socialist governments of the 1980s and 1990s. It was decided to close access to the camp to new arrivals, with the exception of the 'particularly vulnerable', and to demolish the facilities as people left the camp. In fact, the number of occupants continued to fluctuate. The destruction of the Calais Jungle in October 2016 would lead in the following months to an imbalance in the population of the camp at Grand-Synthe: more than 500 Afghan migrants arrived between November 2016 and March 2017 on a site where a large majority were Iraqi Kurds. This led to an increase in tension, and ultimately the total destruction of the camp by a fire in April 2017.

Paris

Paris was sometimes described from the standpoint of migration to the UK as a 'suburb of Calais'. More precisely, Paris was for the migrants a place of arrival, owing to the centralization of the French transport network – a place for getting information, orienting oneself, making contacts, waiting for an opportunity to leave, and sometimes also where the choice was made to remain in France.

The tightening of controls at the port of Calais (since 2000), then around the Channel Tunnel (since 2001), and the closing of the Sangatte centre (in 2002), reinforced this role of a place of waiting and withdrawal in the case of heavy police pressure on the crossing sites.

The Paris encampments, which appeared in the wake of the closing of the Sangatte centre, reflected this role of Paris in the trajectories of migration. They also arose from the policies of successive French governments, with people requiring protection being left in the street (minors, asylum seekers), the saturation of emergency shelter arrangements, and increasingly pronounced forms of segregation at their reception.

Just as at Calais, the policy conducted was one of dispersal by the destruction of encampments, with or without arrests and police harassment. In the course of 2015, with media focus on the arrival of migrants in Europe and the current of solidarity this aroused, the systematic destruction of encampments was accompanied by dispersal to more or less precarious accommodation throughout Île-de-France and even beyond. These dispersal sites gradually became more permanent and were subsequently integrated into the system of Centres d'Accueil et d'Orientation (CAO) – set up to house migrants from the Calais camp after its destruction, then those arriving from the Grande-Synthe camp near Dunkirk.

Following the announcement by the mayor of Paris in spring 2016 that one or more 'refugee camps' would be established in the capital, expulsions from the encampments were no longer accompanied by rehousing in the CAOs. Those expelled were simply thrown onto the street, to the accompaniment of raids and police violence. The media focus on the opening of a 'humanitarian camp' in the northern La Chapelle district, during the six months between its announcement and its actual opening, often hid the brutality of the situation. After the destruction of the Calais Jungle in October 2016, the camp finally opened. A large white and yellow 'bubble' at the entrance, the conception and construction of which had taken a substantial share of the budget, seemed designed to signify a welcoming cocoon. The 'bubble' had one entrance and two exits, one inward and the other outward. Those going out (couples, families with children, women, minors, etc.) were people who did not plan on remaining in France. Sometimes these were offered a housing solution that was more or less precarious, and sometimes they had to spend hours waiting in the bubble, where eating was not allowed. For new entrants, who were only men, the prefecture of police, which had been incapable for years of registering an asylum request in anything less than several months, organized in a few days their fingerprinting and in many cases application of the 'Dublin procedure' without a demand for asylum being registered. There were 400 places, with a maximum stay of ten days while awaiting dispersal to remote centres. Moreover, the lack of places in government accommodation had the effect of slowing down the registering of asylum requests, which in turn led to the centre becoming saturated. Long waiting lines appeared at the entrance, and encampments grew up around it, which were systematically evacuated by the police at the price of new acts of violence, denounced by several of the voluntary organizations, and corroborated by many reports in the early part of 2017.

Belgium and the Netherlands

If migrants crossing to the UK from Belgium and the Netherlands was less publicized than that from France, it is certainly longstanding, and of sufficient scale to have justified a trilateral Franco–Belgian–British meeting on border control in 2002, the measures taken being extended to the Netherlands in 2003 and 2004. On 19 June 2000, a lorry that had left from Rotterdam and crossed via Zeebrugge was discovered at the port of Dover with sixty people on board, fifty-eight of whom were dead from asphyxiation.

The two Belgian ports with ferry connections to the UK were Ostend and Zeebrugge. The existence of encampments at Ostend goes back to 2007. A welfare service, the CAW (Centrum Algemeen Welzijnswerk – 'Centre for Social Work'), made regular rounds and organized a day centre. The harassment and violence on the part of the police were similar to that seen at Calais. The ferry company went bankrupt in 2013, and there has not been a service since then. The focus of crossing attempts thus shifted to Zeebrugge, where encampments started to appear, generally fairly discreet. Police pressure actually remained moderate, so long as there were no tents or huts, and the number of people did not grow too much. Crossing arrangements were also made in service stations inland from the coastline, sometimes giving rise to encampments close to the French border.

In the text of the agreements, the question of control was basically dealt with in connection with the Eurostar trains leaving Brussels for London, while on Belgian public transport heading for the Channel ports the same type of control by appearance was conducted as in France, along with the periodical destruction of encampments. With increasing visibility of the migrant situation, the mayors of the coastal communes, which drew a large share of their income from the tourist trade, demanded repressive measures on the part of the Belgian state, which found expression in a few large-scale police operations. When the southern part of the Calais shantytown was destroyed, in February–March 2016, followed by its final destruction in October, Belgium re-established border controls close to the coast, though these remained more symbolic than effective.

In the Netherlands, given the absence of encampments that made visible the presence of migrants seeking to reach the UK, the question of control remained absent from public debate and the concerns of the voluntary organizations. The only witnesses to it were the migrants themselves.

2

From Sangatte to Calais: inhabiting the 'Jungles'

There is almost nothing left of Sangatte. Yet it is important to speak about it, given that this building and the memory of it remain an abscess that French society and local actors always have in mind when the question is raised of the management of migrants in Calais and the surrounding region. In this chapter we shall re-examine the successive experiences of accommodation for migrants, from the Centre d'Hébergement et d'Accueil d'Urgence Humanitaire at Sangatte (1999–2002) to the Calais Jungle (2015–16), using the perspective and the analytical tools of architecture and urbanism.

Sangatte, 1999–2002

It is quite hard to find precise information about the hangar that had originally been used in constructing the supporting arches for the Channel Tunnel. All that remains today is its imprint on the ground, and the easiest way of gleaning some information is from the aerial photos from Google Earth. On the 2002 photos, you can see a large hangar some 220 metres by 135 on an east–west axis, made up of seven spans. Five of these are 25 metres across, the other two slightly shorter. Its trace is also visible on the IGN map. Of the accessible data, the most detailed documents on Sangatte (from its opening in 1999 to its closure in 2002) are given in Olivier Clochard's 2007 thesis.[1]

What is striking first of all is the great height of the construction, around a dozen metres. The structural frame of 25 metres was extremely wide, and the large red metallic beams that gave a rhythm to the space looked like gigantic machines with nothing human about them. The tents, and the cabins of the construction site (of the prefabricated 'Algeco' type) that were used as living quarters, were strictly aligned on the concrete ground, which was completely flat and horizontal. These cabins and tents were themselves large, able to accommodate a dozen or so people each. Despite their size, they seemed minute in the space of the hangar, which persistently gave an impression of emptiness despite the ever-growing population it housed. Figure 1 presents a plan of the camp in 2002.

Over time, an increasing number of people slept between the cabins and the tents when these became waterlogged, but right to the end, the hangar maintained an extremely well-ordered aspect during the daytime.

Sanitary facilities were installed along the outside walls of the hangar, on platforms bordered on three sides by breeze-block walls in crude primary colours – blue, red, green. The rectangular washbasins and the mirrors above them were lit by neon tubes fixed to the wall, giving them the air of a film set, which was rather incongruous in this austere environment. Despite the hangar offering protection from wind and rain, it was not insulated at all, and the winter temperature was freezing, which made conditions in the tents particularly hard.

At night, the site displayed a rather phantasmagorical aspect. Early in the evening, a white neon light shed a uniform glow throughout the hangar, casting no shadows. The main lights were switched off later, leaving only two spotlights. This left a landscape without colour, composed of silhouettes. The windows of the cabins, each lit by a single neon light, glowed haphazardly in the night, while the darkness of the tents was sometimes enlivened by the isolated flame of a candle. Clochard writes:

> The refugees emphasize how hard it is to rest and sleep; there is a constant echo of sounds. When the spotlights are turned off around midnight, shouts and applause echo in the darkness; then the background brouhaha fades… But this fragile

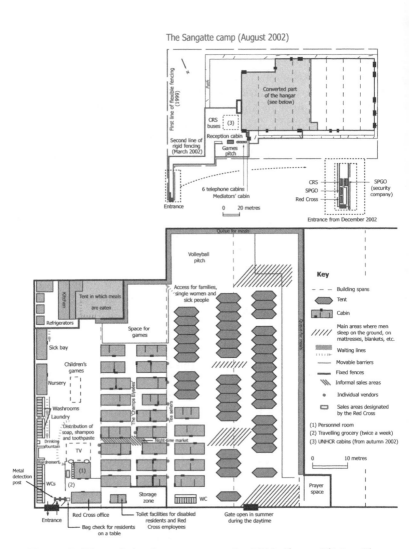

Figure 1. Plan of the Sangatte camp in 2002 (from Olivier Clochard, *Le Jeu des frontières dans l'accès au statut de réfugié*, Université de Poitiers, 2007, p. 252).

quiet can be broken at any moment by a child crying, or the noisy discussion of groups of men sitting on a pathway or walking through the cabins and tents, the shouts of a drunk man.[2]

In summer 2002, the thirty cabins – seven of which were reserved for various services – and thirty-seven tents were spread over an area of one and a half hectares. By the end of 2002, the capacity had increased to 1,200 people, but more than 2,500 appeared at peak periods. Cabins designed for twelve people held up to sixty. Many people slept on the ground between the tents and the cabins.

As we saw above, Sangatte would be closed at the end of 2002, on the decision of interior minister Nicolas Sarkozy.

March 2015: Jungles, camps, squats

Following the closure of the Sangatte camp, the situation in the Calais region became confused and gradually worsened. If the last occupants of the camp saw their situation resolved with a guaranteed passage to England for most of them (see above, p. 20), the gate now closed again behind them, and long years of stagnation lay ahead.

Squats, jungles and camps proliferated, appearing and disappearing as a function of police interventions and the political announcements of various local and national officials, particularly under the presidency of Nicolas Sarkozy (2007–12) and the media soundbites of his short-lived minister of immigration and national identity, Éric Besson. The refugees temporarily settled in abandoned bunkers, or in the holds of boats, until all these shelters were condemned en bloc by the police.[3]

A study of the refugees' various forms of accommodation was conducted in March 2015 by students from the École Nationale Supérieure d'Architecture de Paris-Belleville (ENSAPB). At this time, there were four main sites in the Calais area where refugees congregated: Tioxide, the Galloo squat, the Bois Dubrulle and Leader Price. There were also smaller sites – squats or encampments – of Sudanese, Syrian, Egyptian or Afghan migrants (see figure 2).

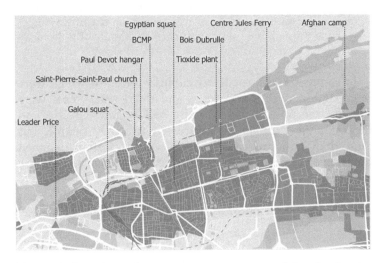

Figure 2. Location of encampments, squats and jungles in the Calais region as of March 2015 (Actes & Cités; ENSAPB; Studio C. Hanappe).

'Leader Price' was the most informal site (see figure 3). Occupied chiefly by Sudanese and Chadians, it was a low-lying and almost marshy field behind the supermarket that lent it its name. The main reason for this choice of site was that it lay inside the loop of exit 42a of the A16 motorway, taken by lorries heading for the Channel Tunnel. This was where so-called '*douggars*' were most frequent – this popular Sudanese Arabic term for tailbacks was applied to all blockages, whether or not they were caused by the migrants; these were always an occasion for general mobilization, spread by social media (SMS, WhatsApp and other messaging apps), and attempts to climb onto the lorries.[4] *Douggars* were also caused by detailed checks on the part of customs officials seeking migrants. The authorities regularly ended up suspending these checks when the tailback grew too long, which created the best opportunity for the migrants.

The Leader Price camp was thus well placed, as well as being in the western suburbs of Calais and just behind a supermarket. Its parking area gave directly onto a field and was visited by several voluntary organizations. Distribution

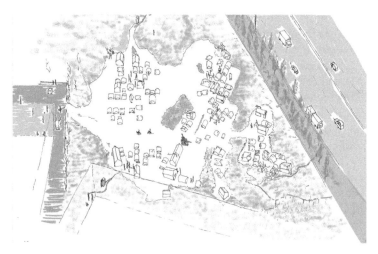

Figure 3. The Leader Price camp in March 2015 (source: ENSAPB; Studio C. Hanappe. Students: Bensaci, Credey, Migliore).

of supplies was frequent, and a large water container was regularly filled up by Médecins du Monde, who made sure it was never empty. On the other hand, there was no mains water supply, and only chemical toilets installed by Médecins du Monde.

Situated in a muddy field, the Leader Price camp gave a real impression of disorder. Of all the Calais shantytowns studied at the time, it was invariably this one that seemed most desolate and badly maintained. Closer examination, however, made it possible to distinguish spaces of life differentiated by time of day. In daylight hours, eight kitchens were installed at different points in the camp, each serving between twelve and twenty people. They each had a wood stove and were the only places to be heated; they served as meeting places throughout the day, and visitors were gladly invited to share tea, warmth and presence on chairs, boxes, or other makeshift seats. These kitchens were constructed out of a collection of pallets and pieces of wood, sometimes covered with grey or black plastic sheets, with a number of lateral openings that could be closed by movable wooden boards to evacuate smoke or let in light.

At night, although there were several tents, people could also sleep in huts that were better sealed, made of pallets covered with several layers of black plastic sheets. These were fixed to the pallet structure by nails or drawing pins pierced through coloured plastic bottle-tops or similar pieces. This technique, 'classic' for shantytowns in France, prevented water leaking in or the plastic tearing. Folds in the sheets were often used for keeping items such as toothbrushes clean and dry.

The floor was also made of pallets. To combat the cold, the cabins were sometimes insulated with blankets, but they had scarcely any ventilation. Besides the dangers of asphyxiation, or at least lack of sufficient oxygen, this is a classic case of a 'bad good idea' in a precarious environment. In fact, the lack of ventilation drove up the humidity, which gave the effect of increased cold, a sensation that was not compensated for by the few degrees of warmth gained.

The camp also contained a few cabins built by volunteers. These had a clearer design and structure, better defined and more rational. They also each had a window and a door.

After the opening of the 'New Jungle' in April 2015, the camp would survive for a few more months, before being evacuated in June the same year.

The Galoo squat was closer to the centre of Calais, in the old industrial districts that had been urbanized in the nineteenth century. On the town side it was bordered by the railway, and occupied a former factory building that had been used for the collection and recycling of iron and other metals. It was officially opened on 12 July 2014, after a demonstration of support for the refugees in response to repeated expulsions (see chapter 1). Right from its opening, this site acquired a particular status, bound up with the strange appearance of the existing factory: a set of five yards in a curve more than 300 metres long, bordered by walls 4 metres high in steel rusted to a deep red colour. The width of the courtyards varied from a few to several dozen metres. One of the court-yards was entirely occupied by a large hangar divided into units, with a traditional roof of dark wooden beams in a complex and repeating pattern. The hangar was lit by lights suspended from the roof, their beams tracing broad swathes through the dark and dusty atmosphere, crisscrossing the spider-web pattern of the beams. The particular atmosphere of this site was increased by the chiaroscuro effect produced by smoke from the fires of the occupants.

In contrast to other sites, the occupation of the Galoo plant was an action entirely conceived and organized by activists and voluntary organizations. Several of these associated this installation with a political and artistic project. The occupation was accompanied by several artistic interventions that would give the site an aesthetic dimension. The Calais artist Loup Blaster painted two gigantic white trees on the rusty steel walls. The giant sycamore, with a lifespan of more than 500 years, was a proud symbol of Eritrea and featured on its banknotes. The long walls of the buildings offered an ideal support for graffitists to draw political-poetic messages: 'LA REVOLTE dessine Aux yeux NOTRE génie d'Histoire' [Revolt makes our spirit of history visible], 'But still, like dust, I'll rise', 'Vous pensez que ce n'est pas légal, nous savons que c'est légitime' [You think it's not legal, we know it's legitimate], 'Le pouvoir est dans la flûte' [The authorities lie], 'Bad things happen because good people do nothing' (see photo 3). As well as these, messages of information and advice to the refugees were pinned up, with contact numbers of people able to assist with particular problems.

Photo 3. Loup Blaster's sycamore in the Galoo squat (photo: Cyrille Hanappe).

But living conditions were not easy. Most of the facilities were in the factory hall, which was the coldest part of the complex. The refugees slept in tents, grouped by affinity (the main nationalities represented were Sudanese, Egyptian, Syrian), and the fires that gave heat and made for community soon created respiratory problems for everyone. The floor was entirely of concrete, sometimes pierced with dangerous holes, and enormous pools of water took weeks to be absorbed. Fort Galoo would be evacuated early in June 2015, at the same time as Leader Price.

Created in the wake of the expulsions of spring 2014, the Bois Dubrulle encampment corresponded most closely to how a 'Jungle' is seen in people's minds. The wood in which it was located had been donated to the town of Calais by a Baron Dubrulle in the late nineteenth century, and lay between the last residential suburbs to the east of Calais and the town's main industrial zone. On an east–west axis along the Rue des Garennes, this zone was some 2 kilometres long and 800 metres wide. The main landmark was the European headquarters and plant of the Tioxide pigment company, which manufactures titanium dioxide – a highly toxic and carcinogenic product, whose bitter-sweet smell strongly marked the environment. The industrial zone also contained hydrocarbon plants (Shell, Kuwait Petroleum) and the Graftech factory, which produced graphite electrodes, and whose tall metal tower punctuates the landscape.

The Tioxide camp was within the industrial zone. To one side of this zone was the Bois Dubrulle, and on the edge of it, separated only by the motorway, the 'New Jungle' would later be established. The zone was well situated for migrants attempting the sea crossing, as it was less than fifteen minutes on foot from the approach roundabout to the port terminus.

Two nationalities were particularly represented in the Bois Dubrulle encampment: Afghans and Ethiopians. There were also some Iranians. The encampment was some 200 by 350 metres on an east–west axis, between the Rue des Garennes and the Route de Gravelines to the south, bordered on this side by houses with gardens behind.

Several hundred persons lived here. Groups congregated in the wood by nationality. Ethiopians were on the southern side, along a path running behind the gardens of the houses on the Route de Gravelines. The Afghans were scattered more in the wood and around the centre, which they shared with a certain number of 'public' and 'common' buildings with several uses: to meet, make purchases, get warm, play sports, pray.

Several types of habitat were present here. Being in a wood, they used its trees as an element of their construction, which were often held together by large blue plastic sheets, giving the site an overall unity. The arrangement of space was marked by a functional differentiation: various platforms, for the most part made of wooden pallets, identified spaces for eating, meeting, cooking and sleeping (see figure 4).

We can look at three dwellings of Afghan migrants established in the Bois Dubrulle. In the first of these, Samir's place, a large tarpaulin hung from the largest trees could be seen

Figure 4. The 'town centre' of the Bois Dubrulle encampment (source: ENSAPB; Studio C. Hanappe. Students: Alves, Carrasco, Lefrançois, Olavarria).

as reminiscent of the *khaïma*, the large Bedouin tent. Here, it unified a space of some 50 square metres. This was tall enough to stand under, and twisted to meet the different functional spaces: there were altogether six platforms, four of these being reserved for sleeping ('igloo'-type tents are erected on each of these), one for meetings and one for meals. The kitchen was right on the ground, with cooking done on a wood fire. Other spaces were used for stacking wood or tinned food. Besides its unifying function, the tarpaulin also protected the whole area from the side, against wind and theft. The same configuration was found at Nowroz's place, with the simple difference that the kitchen space here was located outside the tarpaulin. The final dwelling, Omar's place, known as 'Washington Palace', was more complex and seemed to make better use of the trees, being established around a circular pit some three or four metres in diameter used as an open hearth. Various bits of kitchen and washing equipment were hung from the trees. There were four sleeping units, on each side of the central pit, which was also bordered by a storage unit for crockery. A cooking place was protected against the wind by plastic sheets. Finally, a larger space, itself divided into two smaller ones, enabled the occupants to meet to eat and drink tea when it was raining or too cold. The division between the sub-spaces was marked by a difference in the floor covering. Two mats were positioned on a floor of raised pallets, with chairs grouped around a low table in the other part.

The 'jungle' of Bois Dubrulle was one of the first to disappear at the end of March 2015, when the 'New Jungle' was created. While some of the tents and huts remained in place and were used to store material for the new constructions, a series of night-time arson attacks ended up destroying everything at the end of April.

At the beginning of March 2015, the 'Tioxide camp' was still the largest site where the Calais migrants gathered and lived. In many respects, by its urban structure and complexity, it prefigured what the 'New Jungle' would be. Sheltering between 700 and 900 persons, Sudanese, Eritreans, Egyptians, Syrians and Pakistanis, it was established on a former sports field attached to the Tioxide factory. Occasional patrols organized by the company performed a policing function, forbidding or allowing access to the site. This camp was created at the same time as that in Bois Dubrulle, in the late spring of 2014.

Between the fence (open at several points to allow passage) and the hangar (a former gymnasium with a metal sheeting roof), several huts were erected. The structures were made from bare branches covered with black and blue tarpaulins. They were rudimentary, quite open on the outside, and could be used by traders – hairdressers or sellers of tinned food. One of the huts, quite long but lower and closed, was reserved for sleeping, with black tarpaulins solidly fixed by a network of cords to a few blocks of reinforced concrete that had been found on the site.

On the side of the hangar were two large drawings. One of these referred to Auguste Rodin's sculpture 'The Burghers of Calais'; on grey paper stuck to the metal panel, it depicted a group of six standing migrants, of desperate appearance and clearly unsure where they might go. The other represented a man, who might have been Eritrean, waving in greeting, with a smile that was slight but full of hope. His head was covered in a large blue-green cloth, which fell loosely to his waist. It was signed 'Horor Morione. 2015 – Hope for Everyone' and covered an older graffito of which the only sign remaining were the words 'LaFranceTerDeM' (see photo 4).[5]

Behind the hangar was a second double row of huts. Between two of them was a square hole in the wall, one metre square and some 50 centimetres above the ground. This allowed entry into the building and was its only access. Around 150 tents were packed closely together inside. As the building had no insulation and the weather was cold, fires had been lit and the atmosphere was very smoky. In the heavy pervading silence, the only pale light was that given by the smoked polycarbonate windows in the roof, which cast a luminous halo in the upper part of the hall.

Various buildings had been installed all around the site, in three main groups. These were the most sophisticated of all the jungles, squats and camps in the region. On the north side of the football pitch were predominantly huts. To the east, dwellings clustered around the Coptic church, and on the west side around the mosque and a French-language school (see figure 5).

Photo 4. The Tioxide hangar (photo: Cyrille Hanappe).

The architecture of the mosque was quite particular, demonstrating the great spatial sensitivity of its builders. The asymmetrical plan provided for an entrance sequence that is rarely found in the architecture of traditional mosques, with their centred and symmetrical design, whether Syrian or Sudanese. The positioning of the entrance along the wall was justified only by a choice of architectural proportions. As for the Mihrab, an essential element in mosque architecture that indicates the direction of Mecca, here this was symmetrical with the entrance complex, once again off-centre in the continuation of the long south-eastern façade. By the quality of its composition, the plan of the Tioxide mosque referred to canons of modern architecture and made for a rigorous, asymmetrical and picturesque composition.

The Eritrean church of the Tioxide camp referred to the Coptic Ethiopian design, which itself arose from the Christian Orthodox church. Whereas the original churches were all based on a perfect Greek cross, the typologies that followed evolved in different ways, particularly towards the plan of a Christian basilica. But the most well known of the Byzantine

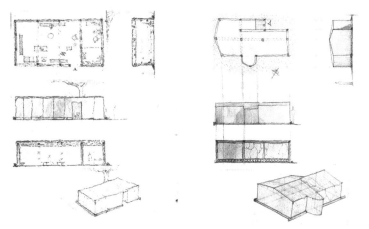

Plan | Cross-section | side view | axonometric projection of the bar   Plan | Cross-section | side view | axonometric projection of the mosque

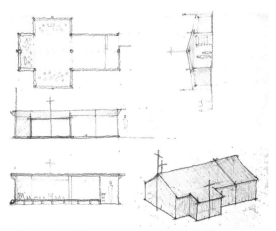

Plan | Cross-section | side view | axonometric projection of the church

Figure 5. Plans of the bar (upper left), the mosque (upper right) and the church (lower) of the Tioxide camp, March 2015 (source: ENSAPB; Studio C. Hanappe. Students: Marino, Sauqué, Stoumpou, Skipsey).

churches is most probably the basilica of Saint Mark in Venice, and it is interesting to compare the plans of these two and note points of convergence. In both cases the choir is slightly shortened in relation to the Greek cross, and the transept extended by the same length cut from the choir. This transept is then extended by a porch, which extends this wing of the building, giving rise to an ambivalence in the design between the two great Christian architectural traditions, a mixed status between Greek and Latin crosses.

Notable among the public facilities at the Tioxide camp were the French-language school and a bar that also served as a restaurant and an assembly room.

The domestic architecture likewise showed a certain number of innovations using recycled products. The solidity of the dwellings was assured by more robust structures with sloping roofs that were well secured to the walls and then descended vertically to the ground. These were made watertight by several layers of tarpaulins covering the whole dwelling, held in place by large nets that were themselves tied to the ground. Tubes or pieces of wood, as well as rocks, guaranteed this fixture. Sheltered entrances allowed shoes to be left in a dry place on entering the dwellings.

As with Bois Dubrulle, the police gave the 1,200 inhabitants of the Tioxide camp notice to quit on 31 March 2015, for evacuation the next morning at 6 am. This was one of the largest expulsions with no rehousing provision conducted in France since 1945. All these people would find themselves in the 'New Jungle', whose opening had been announced a few weeks earlier.

April 2015 to October 2016: the Jungle or 'the art of building towns'[6]

On 3 September, *Le Monde* announced an unexpected turn on the part of the French government. Twelve years after Sangatte, on whose closure there had been broad consensus among the country's political class, Natacha Bouchart, the mayor of Calais, declared that she had received a green light from the interior ministry to create a reception centre.[7] For several months, while the parameters of this centre were being worked out until it finally opened in January 2015 (under the name of the Centre Jules Ferry), the question of accommodation was assiduously avoided, and remained a collective un-thought, to say the least. Only with an article in the regional daily *La Voix du Nord* on 7 March 2016 was the news announced that 'conscious that the evacuation of squats is necessary, Natacha Bouchart has confirmed, to make up for this, the impending establishment of a temporary reception site located close to the Centre Jules Ferry: a large surface that will enable those migrants wishing to cross to England to "halt", but also allow them a better exchange with international bodies, away from people-smugglers.'[8] On 24 March, the same paper reported that this site, then known as the 'dunes zone', had seen its first arrivals take possession: 'Around 25 migrants, of Afghan, Pakistani or Sudanese origin, have already pitched their tents in this new space made available by the town hall... Natacha Bouchart and the sub-prefect of Calais, Denis Gaudin, had already "encouraged migrants to use this place for themselves" at the beginning of March.'[9]

Formation of a town

In Calais, therefore, we had the *garenne* [warren], the *lande* [heath], and then the *jungle*. A town is initially a site. In this case, its geometry was clearly bounded by paths that gave it a clear and well-proportioned form. Despite being exposed to the dangers of the adjacent factory (a so-called Seveso zone, classified as an industrial risk), this did not present any problem in everyday life. The poplars alongside the Centre Jules Ferry and the Chemin des Dunes to the north and east, and the motorway embankment to the west, limited the effect of the most violent winds. The ground was entirely on compressed sandy soil, offering an extremely stable basis for constructions of all kinds, while quite rapidly absorbing excess water and thus limiting muddy zones. A feature of the site was the existence of a large body of water, nearly 300 metres long by 60 metres wide, which cut the site in two, dividing its northern and southern sections. There were three main access points to the Lande. One was at the end of the Rue des Garennes, exit 2 on the link road connecting the A16 motorway with the ferry terminal. The two others were along the Chemin des Dunes, at the south-east and north-east of the site.

Where the Rue des Garennes enters the site, it very soon turns into a track, ending at a T-junction after some 50 metres, where it divides into a northern and a southern spur. To the north, the track heads north-west for about 250 metres before reaching a large sandy stretch extending to the Chemin des Dunes; this is some 300 metres wide and scattered with small hillocks, the tallest of which is about 10 metres high at its centre. There are also low points where water accumulates on rainy days and takes a few days to disappear. All around the sandy area, to the north and west, is an area of thorny bushes that are almost impenetrable, apart from a winding motocross path on the side of the motorway whose arabesques are scatted with the cartridges of hunting guns (subsequently also with a high density of excrement).

To the south, the road from the end of the Rue des Garennes disappears after some 50 metres, giving way to a number of paths that ultimately became the streets and roads of the urban zone. One of these, initially not distinguished in any way from the others, ends up after a few detours joining the access route to the south-east of the site. This would become the main business street of the Jungle. See figure 6.

The southern part

In October 2015, the southern part contained four main zones of habitation. The first of these ran from the entrance on the Rue des Garennes along the main road, then crossing the site diagonally towards the Chemin des Dunes south-east of the *lande*. This road was initially for business, conducted almost exclusively by Afghans, and later marked by the presence of the Eritrean church and the houses that went with this. The road then ran in a gully (one of the few muddy parts of the whole Jungle), and only reappeared close to where it reached the Chemin des Dunes, with the École Laïque and the group of tents and caravans brought by the No Border activists and intended for Kurdish families.

The second major inhabited zone developed patchily from the Chemin des Dunes; it was populated mainly by Sudanese,

Forest

Lake

Figure 6. Calais Jungle, October 2015 (source: ENSAPB. Teachers: Aquilino, Chombart de Lauwe, Hanappe).

who developed complex groups of dwellings here. The third zone, less populated, was a small wood to the south-west that was fairly hidden and hard to access, protected from all the bustle that prevailed elsewhere. Finally, many people lived in the buffer zone between the wood and the main road.

Entering the Jungle from the Rue des Garennes gave a strong sensation. There would be people moving in every direction, and right along the road were businesses of all kinds – restaurants, grocers, hotels, sellers of phone cards, etc. Electricity generators, TVs, and sound systems playing Indian pop songs in the restaurants, created a lively soundscape, while the comings and goings of trucks of the international NGOs, the utility vehicles of volunteers, the water-trucks that emptied the few toilets and distributed water, gave the fleeting impression of a frenetic city in southeast Asia.

The restaurants and shops were kept by Afghans. They had evocative names (e.g., 'Kaboul Restaurant', 'AFG Flag', 'Salam Bar'), and their signboards, created by talented street artists, gave a particularly rich image at this crossroads of different urban cultures.

The restaurants were the largest buildings in the Jungle, some more than 100 square metres. Their structures, rational but always extremely under-sized, were built from pieces of industrial timber that allowed a larger span: up to 4 metres, with heights more than 3 metres. The construction sites employed up to a dozen workers, and restaurateurs needed an investment of €5,000 to launch their business.

As with the makeshift shacks, waterproofing was ensured by black tarpaulins secured by pieces of wood or by nails through plastic bottle-tops. These tarpaulins stretched from the roof to the walls, and were then fixed to the ground, using small piles of sand and heavier branches as ballast. The walls and roofs were insulated within by covers or duvets hung from the structure.

The interior architecture of the restaurants (see figure 7) was invariably marked by a spatial division between the cooking space and the dining area, separated by a bar that served as a sales counter. In the dining area, there was almost always a wide bench running along the walls. This would be covered with cloth, and wide enough to sit on horizontally, seated tailor-fashion with a plate, or else lying on your side

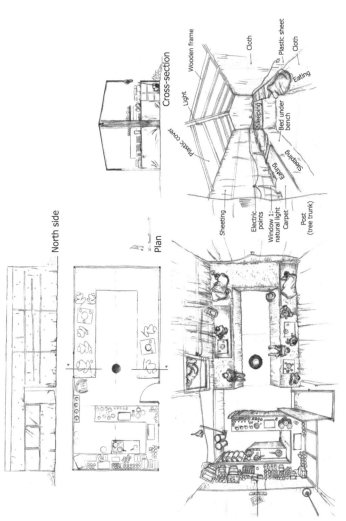

Figure 7. Afghan restaurant, Calais Jungle, October 2015 (source: ENSAPB. Teachers: Aquilino, Chombart de Lauwe, Hanappe. Students: Frikha, Guarin, Pujole, Tumbarello).

with a low portable table opposite. In the largest restaurants, there would also be a 'European-style' zone with tables and chairs. Like the dining areas, the kitchens opened onto the road, enabling them to present the dishes figuring on the menu and sell them directly. The restaurants also served as accommodation for their owners, and sometimes also as a hotel for new arrivals.

The shops, for their part, were simpler, yet striking by the impression of profusion that they gave. Accessible only from the street, they were impossible to enter, and presented a large façade, either glazed or with a grille, and a small opening for the purpose of transactions. On every wall, on the ground and hanging from the ceiling would be tins of food, drinks, phone chargers, etc. At the end of this quarter was the large Eritrean church, surrounded by a few dwellings of fellow nationals, who included several women (see figure 8, a house of eight women within a small courtyard of Eritrean refugees made up of six permanent dwellings and a large tent).

In the wood at the south-west of the site the dwellings were far more informal, groups of tents and very precarious shacks gathered around a fire. It was extremely damp here, and there was so little light that even in the daytime mobile phones had to be used for lighting, according to the inhabitants. Out of a concern for protection, the tents and huts were grouped extremely closely together and often touched. One of the huts we found abandoned, which was a rare occurrence, as no one wanted to sleep there on account of the smell. Here the people were mainly Afghan, with a few Pakistanis.

Other groups had settled around the wood. Pakistanis, Iraqi Kurds and Syrians had established in similar fashion small groups of shacks and tents around a fire that was generally sheltered by a tarpaulin. These groupings were separate from one another, a few dozen metres apart and divided by thick vegetation. In contrast with other zones of the Jungle, this was not an urban situation but more of a woodland way of life. In this zone there were hardly any of the prefabricated cabins provided by the voluntary organizations. Instead, a technique was used that was not often found elsewhere, constructing side walls for the huts with fencing grilles from building sites.

The Sudanese were almost all settled on the east of the site, along the Chemin des Dunes, from the south to the north

Figure 8. House of a group of Eritrean women, Calais Jungle, October 2015 (source: ENSAPB. Teachers: Aquilino, Chombart de Lauwe, Hanappe. Students: Frikha, Guarin, Pujole, Tumbarello).

Plan

Cross-section CC

South-east side

Cross-section AA

Cross-section BB

between the Route de Gravelines and the Centre Jules Ferry, and in pockets of urban development extending towards the inner part of the camp. A hillock of sand and earth, between one and three metres high, separated this part from the Chemin des Dunes, allowing the people settled here to be both protected and close to a major communication axis: the Chemin des Dunes directly connected to the Centre Jules Ferry, it was lit up at night, and a preferred delivery place for individual donors and NGOs.

Urban development occurred along winding paths beside the groups of dwellings. Whenever they were consulted, the majority of Sudanese maintained that they had no special desire to go to the UK. This was perhaps the reason why their dwellings were the most elaborate, complex and large (see figure 9). Combining prefabricated or hand-built houses

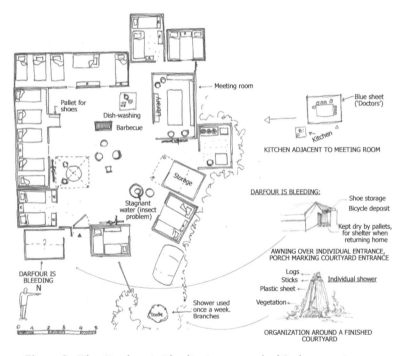

Figure 9. The 'Darfour is Bleeding' courtyard of Sudanese migrants (source: ENSAPB. Teachers: Aquilino, Chombart de Lauwe, Hanappe. Students: Baïram, Gkiola, Hanart, Vilquin).

with made-to-measure communal spaces, they were grouped into courtyards whose uses were very carefully regulated. Besides sleeping quarters, there would regularly be a kitchen, a storage space for food, a covered space with furniture to sit on for communal meals, and sometimes even a further space to pass the time during the day. The buildings for sleeping were low, in order to conserve heat, and you entered by a tiny 'hall' equipped with shelves on which shoes could be left. They were all covered with black plastic sheets that gave protection from daylight. The kitchens were tall and well ventilated, slightly apart so as to limit the risk of fire, while food would be stored in a quite well-lit building, carefully closed to give protection from pests. The 'meeting rooms' were also tall and well lit, yet protected from the wind, and equipped with a small library and a large table. The courtyards themselves were conceived as rooms in the open air, with their hearth and spaces for reception and exchange. The sanitary facilities, essentially showers, were outside the courtyards, in the interstices between the urban spaces. These showers were generally in a man-high wooden structure, with a footprint of less than a square metre. The floor would be made from a pallet, making it possible to wash here sheltered from the wind and other people, while keeping your feet out of the mud.

The northern part

In October 2015, the northern section was far less occupied than the southern. The business axis that started from the Route des Garennes continued as far as the stretch of sand that then had only a few dozen huts. As in the southern part, the Sudanese were along the Chemin des Dunes as far as the Centre Jules Ferry to the north. The Syrians, in a hurry to leave, were settled in tents along the motorway and on a small hillock to the north of the stretch of sand that was known as the 'Syrians' road'. A member of the Bedouin community, a stateless minority from Kuwait, occupied a hut built by Secours Catholique.

Only after the destruction of the southern zone, in March 2016, did the northern part of the Jungle undergo a real development, as the only urbanized zone remaining. The increased density, combined with the reduction in area (37 per cent of the original) would lead to a far more intense usage of the site. Groupings by nationality were temporarily lost in a mixing that would generate tension between everyone.

In the course of summer 2016, this northern zone urbanized northwards across the bushes. But the existing tensions, the police attacks that had become constant, and the increased density, meant that the atmosphere would never be as flourishing as it had been in the southern zone. The trauma of demolition did not prevent the blossoming of a few moments of architectural grace, but the fear instilled by the constant attacks from the authorities caused a great deal of damage to the quality of life. There were scarcely any constructions here apart from the cabins of the voluntary organizations. The groups of dwellings were more formal, closer together, and more enclosed. The courtyards, when they existed, were restricted to more reduced spaces, and the fears created by different tensions (police harassment, proximity, competition between nationalities) meant that they were more enclosed. Very often they were protected by walls several metres high, which blocked outside glances and visual interchange.

None the less, the northern part would remain until the end the last urban portion of the Calais Jungle. This is where more than 8,000 persons would reside (deducting from the 10,000 counted by the Auberge des Migrants the 1,500 in the containers of the Centre d'Accueil Provisoire and 500 at the Centre Jules Ferry), on an ever-decreasing surface, reduced to around 10 hectares by October 2016. The density then was 800 people per hectare, equivalent to 80,000 per square kilometre – a world record, double that of Cairo or Manila, which are generally seen as the highest in the world.

The commons

Throughout the life of the Jungle, a number of 'common buildings' (*bâtiments communs*) appeared. The term 'commons' is preferable to 'public services',[10] both because of the lack of public investment in the Jungle, and because of the way in which these sites were managed, which was communal and voluntary. The international NGOs (Médecins du Monde, Solidarités International, Médecins Sans Frontières), along with many voluntary organizations and individuals from France and northern Europe, came to the site and installed a certain amount of infrastructure without any brief from the state: schools, churches, mosques, communal kitchens, libraries, an art school, a kindergarten, a theatre, a centre for young people. We shall return to the social life of these places in the following chapter.

Together with these buildings went interventions by artists, particularly in the form of street art, which brilliantly captured the quality of life in the Jungle. Banksy is the most famous of these, but several others worked on the signboards of shops and restaurants, on signposts, on certain particular buildings and in the concrete entrance tunnel, the site for many such artistic expressions. In December 2015 the 'Art in the Jungle' collective offered an art workshop that would bequeath a number of elements, such as its 'hotspots', a kind of stylized brazier, used also as Wi-Fi connection points. Certain places, such as the École Laïque on the Chemin des Dunes, were the focus of these interventions, some of which were both children's games and relaxation areas.

Bit by bit, a community and a public space were formed by self-management; a town was born, whose components all followed the same processes as any other town in formation, but at a crazily accelerated pace. This town began to focus the attention of the whole world, which could well appreciate how it was both prophetic and catastrophic in character, marvellous and wretched, utopian and dystopian.

This was clearly too much for the French state. At a meeting between the voluntary organizations and two government representatives in December 2015, the latter expressed 'a sentiment of great disquiet in relation to the self-management drift of the shantytown'. The demolition of the Calais Jungle would be a slow and systematic process, implacable and proceeding in stages.

The architecture of non-reception

The involvement of the state in terms of the architecture of reception amounted to three actions: the creation of a daytime reception centre, of a container camp, and of a no man's land.

The Jules Ferry day centre was the first of these three acts. As we have seen, it was established at the beginning of 2015, in a former leisure centre abandoned by the municipality. Four hundred places in prefabricated cabins were reserved for women and children, but a year later no less than 1,179 children would be counted in this establishment, including 1,022 single minors, some 700 of these still without a guardian in August 2016.

Then came the Centre d'Accueil Provisoire (CAP). Less than six months after having proclaimed his 'tolerance' of the free installation of migrants in the Jungle, the then prime minister, Manuel Valls, announced in September 2015 his desire to create a 'tent camp' on the same site of *La Lande*. This would end up being a container camp. The voluntary organization La Vie Active, which already managed the Centre Jules Ferry, was appointed to manage this on 4 October 2015, and plans began to appear in the course of that month. There was at no point any mention of an architect, and, although a construction permit was posted up in the camp, it is unclear on what basis a construction of such size (more than 4,440 square metres) could have been authorized on the northern zone. Legally, this was a 'sector dedicated to remarkable natural or characteristic spaces of the littoral, where light equipment may be installed under very particular conditions, designed in such a way as to make possible a return of the site to the natural state and the exclusion of any form of dwelling.'

The architecture of the CAP was reminiscent of a dystopian installation of the 1970s (see photo 5). On a site that was rectangular and entirely fenced, 125 containers, uniformly white, on one or two levels, were strictly aligned along two axes. These ran in a west-north-westerly direction, forming roads that attracted the coldest prevailing winds, even accelerating these in this very exposed seaside zone. Their proximity and orientation meant that the roads were in the shade for the greater part of the day and did not see the sun at all in winter. The public space was reduced to what remained between the containers, a uniform stretch of pebbles scarcely broken by the metal access steps. In each of the containers, which were heated, twelve people slept on bunk beds along the outside walls. Here again, no personal appropriation was tolerated – not even a poster or photo.

Photo 5. The container camp (Centre d'Accueil Provisoire), Calais Jungle, October 2016 (photo: Sara Prestianni).

Less often mentioned, the third architectural act of the public authorities consisted in a no man's land adjacent to the Jungle. Empty spaces were created, though these were re-appropriated in various ways by the Jungle's inhabitants. The first space cleared was a 100-metre strip around the Route de Gravelines and the motorway link leading to the port. This strip was then extended, in March 2016, to the whole of the southern sector, leaving only four small communal buildings. The wide sandy zone thus created, however, would remain occupied by the Jungle inhabitants, as it offered an open space at a time when the shantytown was experiencing the saturation described above.

A few weeks after its evacuation and clear-up in March 2016, the southern zone would see the appearance of a luxurious and uniform vegetation of perennial plants with yellow flowers, which some people attributed to the action of volunteers. For several months, this stretch acquired the fantastical and peaceful aspect of a limitless cloud of yellow pistils floating on dishevelled dark green leaves, with the Eritrean church and the École Laïque seeming to appear above these, and behind them the motorway leading to the promised land.

A football pitch was constructed at the centre and would be the site of a number of matches between mixed teams of volunteers and migrants of all nationalities. A red truck equipped with a Wi-Fi aerial came every day and put up a number of games tables at which the refugees could play backgammon or chess.

As for the no man's land bordering the motorway to the north, this acquired the function of a public space for all: a space of exchange but also of friction and even fights, a space for games ranging from cricket for the Afghans to football for the Sudanese, filled at the end of the day by everyone seeking a bit of fresh air, and some escape from the density and effervescence of the shantytown.

The shantytown was a town

In the light of the camp, the shantytown and the no man's land, it is highly likely that the Calais Jungle may one day be seen as a caricature of the opposition between two conflicting models for the town of the twenty-first century.

Authoritarian order, tight security, rigidity, endless controls, the prohibition of personal activities, the negation of individuality – the container camp gave expression to a totalitarian vision of society in which the possibilities of personal emancipation are almost zero. Expensive, and generating a healthy profit for its constructors, it was ordered directly by the state from a company that benefited from a situational rent, built from kit to the detriment of manual labour and the profit of generic manufactured product (an exportable camp model, according to its promoters), thus exemplary on all these points of the economic model that emerged in the 2010s.

In contrast to this, the shantytown was disorganized, intuitive and inefficient, and exposed its denizens to an acute level of certain risks. It exhibited an aesthetic of disorder and recycling, a logic of makeshift and cooperation, manual work and building energy. It was also ecological, social, inscribed in a human and economic fabric capable of mobility. In its conception it seemed, as Camillo Sitte would wish, 'following the school of Nature and the Ancients in the domain of urbanism as in others'.[11]

As a town of migrants, refugees fleeing misery and war, the Jungle would have more than 10,000 inhabitants. An urban life organized itself, with its restaurants, meeting places, religious buildings, sites of culture and exchange, schools – as we shall go on to see. An architecture was elaborated there in the face of adversity and precariousness, yet with its own novelty. An architecture of mobility, of the ephemeral and the uncertain, bound up with the functions and cultures of different peoples, notably the generous 'yards' of the Sudanese (see figure 9) or the large and welcoming Afghan restaurants (figure 7). Also a knowledgeable architecture, as when the Eritreans constructed a broad and tall church ('prepared' a few months earlier by the one in the Tioxide encampment – cf. figure 5), when the Nigerian Zimako Jones built the 'secular school of the Chemin des Dunes', or when an association of young British architects built a kindergarten, reminiscent of a building by Le Corbusier.

3

A sociology of the Jungle: everyday life in a precarious space

How was day-to-day life organized in the precarious space of the Calais Jungle? As an informal place of coexistence between communities with different cultures, languages and trajectories, social relations were sometimes tense in the Jungle. At an everyday level, however, a certain equilibrium came into being. How did this happen, and what was the role of the voluntary organizations and public authorities in this equilibrium?[1] As shown by the history and development of the Calais shantytown camp described above, this did not just depend on the migrants, in a kind of 'spontaneous generation' – an impression corroborated by the repeated use of the term 'Jungle' to denote the place, caricaturing its exceptional and exotic character. It was actually a triangular relation, between: the migrants who lived there and adapted to it without having chosen it; the public authorities (municipality, prefecture, government), who acted in different ways but always strongly marked by hostility; and the fabric of voluntary organizations and ordinary citizens who mobilized in the name of solidarity and sought to compensate for the insufficiencies of state-sponsored reception schemes.

Society under precarious conditions

To understand how the everyday life of this society was organized, established as it was in precarious conditions, it is necessary to start from the arrangement of the site that has just been described, and the juxtaposition of different spaces between which people circulated without any institutional framework. Three areas found themselves under different 'jurisdictions'. First of all there was the Centre Jules Ferry, which in a sense was the 'origin' of everything else, being the daytime reception centre opened by the state, and managed by a non-profit contractor; the shantytown developed around this. The centre distributed meals (some 7,000 per day: 3,500 breakfasts and 3,500 lunches in summer 2016); there was also accommodation for 400 women and children.

The second area was the shantytown, an informal encampment gradually organized by the migrants with the assistance of individuals, voluntary organizations and NGOs (in September 2015, Médecins Sans Frontières erected shelters; then, after a decision by the administrative tribunal, ACTED installed water points, toilets, roadways and lighting). This was the 'Jungle' in the strict sense. The third area, the Centre d'Accueil Provisoire or CAP [Temporary Accommodation Centre], represented the alternative to the shantytown proposed by the state, and was managed by La Vie Active (which already managed the Centre Jules Ferry). The CAP was made up of containers, and could house up to 1,500 people.

In summer 2016, 20 per cent of the total number living on the site were housed in the facilities provided by the state, in the Centre d'Accueil Provisoire or the Jules Ferry Centre for women and children.[2] Eighty per cent of those living on the site thus lived in the shantytown section, where the voluntary organizations, NGOs and individual helpers provided services in the absence of any direct intervention by the public authorities.

The Calais shantytown was originally formed by migrants in transit to the UK and blocked at the border, but in the course of a few months it became a focal point for new precarious arrivals, who, though wishing to seek asylum in France, had no other housing solution than this site where members of their community had already gathered. In summer 2016, the main nationalities represented were Afghans and Sudanese, who formed more than two-thirds of the total number of migrants on the site. Among other substantial groups were Eritreans, Ethiopians, Pakistanis, Syrians and

Iraqis. The Jungle population may be interpreted as expressing a certain state of global conflicts, but it also reflected the different migration routes and their fluctuations.

The precise number of inhabitants on the site, and the composition of this population, has been subject to debate, with very different estimates produced by the voluntary organizations and the prefecture, all the more so as the number of weekly arrivals was very variable, with a substantial turnover due to frequent movement between Calais, the Paris encampments around the La Chapelle quarter, and the various sites of crossing attempts, at Norrent-Fontes/Isbergues, Steenvoorde/ Hazebrouck, Grande-Synthe/Dunkirk, Cherbourg and in Belgium.

To challenge the inadequacy of the arrangements offered by the public authorities, volunteers had to produce precise figures, and therefore conducted headcounts that give a portrait of the Jungle population and its development over time. In summer 2016, the site had between 6,901 and 9,106 persons – the lower figure being that of the prefecture as of 17 August 2016, and the higher one that of Auberge des Migrants/Help Refugees, between 6 and 10 August. This figure was higher than the first count conducted by the voluntary organizations at the end of February 2016, which had shown 3,451 persons in the northern zone alone, before the demolition of the southern zone. During the summer of 2016, more than twice the number of refugees were living packed intensely together on a space reduced by half.

The inhabitants of the Jungle were mainly men. In summer 2016, 200 women were housed in the Centre Jules Ferry; a few women also lived in the shantytown part of the site, most often with a partner or family, though sometimes in single-sex groups. It is hard to arrive at a precise number, but women certainly represented less than 5 per cent of the total population of the Calais camp in 2016. They made up a larger share in some smaller encampments in the region, for example at Norrent-Fontes where there was a particularly higher proportion of young Eritrean women; or at Grande-Synthe, which housed a higher proportion of families. The counts made by voluntary organizations showed 865 minors on the Calais site in August 2016, of whom 80 per cent were unaccompanied. Most of them were adolescents from Eritrea, Afghanistan and Sudan; some were children separated from their families in the course of their journey, or who had left with an elder brother or cousin. The youngest was eight years old. A substantial number of them had families in the UK, which entitled them to apply for asylum there. However, given the lack of social and legal support, the majority of these minors were unable to make such applications.

Unaccompanied minors became a more sensitive issue as they made up a growing share of the camp population during the summer of 2016. From an estimate of around 400 in February of that year, these rose to nearly 1,300 by October (see photo 6). Responsibility for minors comes under the remit of the child protection services, whose structures were inadequate both for the number of minors concerned, and for their migratory trajectory. A youth shelter run by France Terre d'Asile in the town of Saint-Omer (some 50 kilometres from Calais, with 45 places) offered emergency accommodation, and cared for those wishing to seek asylum in France. The CAP in the Calais Jungle dedicated 200 places in the containers for unaccompanied minors, without any special arrangement or adequate support (just two carers), contrary

Photo 6. Children in the Calais Jungle, February 2016 (photo: Sara Prestianni).

to the child protection rules. A project for 70 additional places was under study in autumn 2016 but was never completed.

The majority of unaccompanied minors lived in the shanty-town, sometimes in a group of young people, sometimes with an 'uncle' granting protection, a service that was not always free and brought with it the risks of exploitation and abuse.[3] Since assistance from the public authorities was quite inadequate, outsiders, whether individuals, members of voluntary organizations or NGOs, played a major role in taking day-to-day responsibility for these unaccompanied minors.

Domestic organization in the Jungle's small dwelling units (tents, huts) varied substantially according to the make-up of the group (families or peer groups), and depending on their stronger or weaker connection with volunteers, who sometimes joined these groups and lived with them.

Abu Ali's family, for example, were from Syria, made up of the father and mother, a son aged 20, a daughter aged 15 and a son of 13. The women decided against going to live in the Centre Jules Ferry, in order to stay with their family. They had settled close to the Syrian quarter, and arranged themselves like a traditional Arab household, with a number of rooms grouped around a central courtyard: a sitting-room/bedroom, a kitchen corner, one for washing, and another bedroom also used for storage. Meals were cooked and eaten here, sometimes brought in from outside by one of the men of the house, or else by volunteers. Yet, because this hut was relatively comfortable in relation to other shelters, it also served a wider community function. Syrian women from the Jungle would meet there, as well as volunteers bringing donations or giving lessons to the girl. She herself never went outside, her parents fearing the insecurity of the Jungle.

Anouar was a Sudanese aged 25. On his arrival at Calais, he had spent several nights sleeping in the 'Sudanese tent', which served as a reception place for new arrivals. He made friends with another Sudanese of his own age, also from the Omdurman district of Sudan. This man suggested that they share his hut, as his former room-mate had crossed to England. This hut had a very low ceiling, and just a single room with a raised bed on which both men slept. Being unable to cook in the hut, they went to the distributions organized at the Centre Jules Ferry, or by the voluntary organizations' kitchens in the shantytown. Anouar spent some time with other Sudanese who had a more spacious hut, with a courtyard outside where it was possible to cook. He rapidly abandoned any attempt to cross to England, and spent a great deal of his time at the Chemin des Dunes school, where he set himself to learn French. His friend Ahmed, however, continued to make night-time attempts at crossing, and also stayed regularly at the Norrent-Fontes encampment, close to the motorway service station inland from Calais. Rather than forming a domestic unit, the two friends simply shared a tiny space, spending as much time as possible outside.

Ali was an Afghan aged 26. He lived alone in a hut that he bought from another Afghan, who had left for the container camp. His hut was tiny, but he had a stove and cooked here, most often with a friend who lived in the neighbouring hut. He spent the greater part of the daytime outside the hut, in one of the various restaurants that showed Bollywood films.

Joumana, finally, was a Filipina aged 30, who fled Libya where she was born. As an unaccompanied woman, she did not feel safe in the Jungle, yet did not want to stay in the Centre Jules Ferry for women and children. After meeting a family of Malaysian volunteers who had established a community kitchen in the shantytown, 'Kitchen in Calais',[4] she decided to live with them. In exchange for help in preparing meals, she stayed in a caravan in the courtyard of this kitchen, along with three other refugees who also assisted. She integrated into the life of this group and only rarely left the Jungle. The kitchen received many visitors, who came with donations or to lend a hand, and these visits gave a rhythm to her everyday life.

Settling in the shantytown

As a space marginal to the state control of individuals, the shantytown made possible a form of community self-organization, marked by relations of solidarity but also of competition and sometimes of violence. All refugee camps display cleavages between population groups, yet at Calais, in contrast to camps situated in the countries adjacent to conflict zones, the heterogeneity of the population was particularly great, which could cause difficulties of communication and coexistence, in exceptional cases escalating to confrontation.[5] On a daily basis, however, relations were facilitated by modes of regulation among migrants and by the intervention of individuals, voluntary organizations and NGOs providing various services.

Communities in the shantytown divided themselves geographically into neighbourhoods, more or less homogeneous according to the availability of space. People congregated as much as possible by ethnic and linguistic group. The shantytown thus developed distinct neighbourhoods – Pashtun (from Afghanistan and Pakistan), Oromo (from Ethiopia), Kurd (from Iraq, Iran), etc. A shelter was often inhabited by several persons, and close to other shelters with whom it shared meals and protection. Among the Sudanese, for example, groupings of ten to fifteen individuals shared a common kitchen and took turns in preparing meals, as shown by the example of the 'Darfour is Bleeding' courtyard (cf. figure 9 in chapter 2). These groupings were facilitated by direct or indirect acquaintance based on a kinship connection or geographical proximity of origin.

Newcomers could count on the help of members of their community who were already established, and of volunteers attending the site. Some communities organized a regular reception system with the help of voluntary organizations. For example, the Sudanese had a large tent, erected by the organizations, that served as first shelter for newcomers and housed an average of fifty people, sometimes more. The Afghan restaurants could also put up newcomers, until they found somewhere more permanent to sleep. The association Auberge des Migrants established a distribution point for newcomers, the 'Welcome caravan', which gave out sleeping bags and tents.

In the early phase of the shantytown, from spring to winter 2015, it was possible to clear and flatten spaces on the natural site known as the *lande* ('moor'), so as to erect shelters there. Voluntary organizations had a certain room for manoeuvre in helping migrants put up a tent or a hut away from the flooded zone, using earth-moving equipment and bringing caravans onto the site. The successive decisions on partial demolition reduced the available area and put an end to the possibility of improving the site, just as the population there was increasing. In spring and summer 2016, the number of weekly arrivals was estimated at 500, despite a substantial turnover, as mentioned above.

The strong pressure on space that followed the partial demolition of March 2016 increased the difficulty of community life, often desired for the purpose of protection and mutual support, given the lack of room available and the growing scarcity of wooden shelters. Besides, given the ban since spring 2016 on bringing construction material onto the site, the newcomers had to make do with tents, or else resort to the clandestine 'housing market' to rent or buy shelters. In summer 2016, a wooden hut sold for around €150, and a caravan for about €350. Access to certain places could be restricted by an 'entrance fee' imposed by individuals who were unofficial leaders, smugglers or their accomplices. At Grande-Synthe, too, in the 'humanitarian camp' established by the municipality, the organization that managed the site had to wage a constant battle against the grip of smugglers on the shelters constructed for refugees. Relations of solidarity between communities were combined with relations of power, with the result that the encampment, a preferred alternative to solitary wandering, could also be a place of violence.

The state facility of container housing, established at Calais to offer decent and secure habitation, had only 1,500 places. It was initially designed as a 'temporary' shelter, before migrants were directed to other structures outside of the region (the Centres d'Accueil et d'Orientation, scattered all over France), or even a permanent housing solution for those wishing to seek asylum in France (the Centres d'Accueil pour Demandeurs d'Asile [Accommodation Centres for Asylum Seekers]). At the time of its opening in January 2016, the container camp met with some reticence on the part of the migrants; this was due to the biometric control of entries, a reminder of police fingerprinting, and to certain constraints on everyday life such as forced cohabitation (the association La Vie Active decided on the allocation of places in the container), or again to the lack of space to do one's own cooking. Despite this, the available places were gradually filled. The anticipated rotation did not take place because the accommodation system for asylum seekers in France was insufficient and suffered from organizational defects, and the Temporary Accommodation Centre was rapidly saturated. In summer 2016, the waiting list had grown to several hundred persons, and only the most vulnerable were given priority.

Economic and social life

The particular character of the Jungle in 2015–16 in relation to previous encampments in Calais or other encampments in northern France was its specific stability and autonomy. Away from the town centre (more than 30 minutes' walk), the shantytown developed its own services and its own economic activity. The number of restaurants, food shops and other businesses (barber/hairdresser, vegetable and clothing stalls, etc.) was the most striking sign of this: 72 businesses were counted in July 2016, when the prefecture took legal proceedings to close them (see photo 7).

Restaurants were the most visible part of the shantytown's everyday economic life, and favoured spaces for its social life. They were places where communities mixed, and meeting

Photo 7. A hairdressing salon, Calais Jungle, December 2015 (photo: Sara Prestianni).

points between volunteers and migrants. It was possible to eat here, to drink tea, charge your mobile, watch a Bollywood film or a video. In the restaurants, one could spend time in a less confined space than that of the shelters, and use the electricity provided by generators. Some became famous spots in the Calais Jungle: the Kabul Café, a gathering place for volunteers and NGO workers, hosted the first community meetings on the site, before being destroyed in March 2016 with the demolition of the southern zone; the White Mountain was particularly famous for its bakery and its film programme; the Three Idiots was so popular with the volunteers that it became a musical stage for weekend concerts.

The cost of opening a restaurant in the shantytown was certainly lower than in Calais, but nonetheless required a starting capital both to purchase material and to build a construction of sufficient size. For those who had not arrived when the shantytown started, it was often necessary to either buy or rent space from the former occupants. Almost all the businesses were run by Afghans or Pakistanis, who had invested their savings in this activity (sometimes the result of a former migration to England) and employed other refugees, often from their own region or city, to work there. There was an informal housing market, with prices depending on the commercial interest of the site, the main arteries of the shantytown being the most prized. A business site would fetch anything between €2,000 and €6,000. But this value could suddenly collapse, as these were by definition precarious constructions that could be destroyed on the order of the public authorities, or as a result of fires, whether deliberate or not, that were frequent and devastating.

These businesses offered a relatively lucrative activity in comparison with the general standard of living in the shantytown. By handling money, the traders could also act as intermediaries in various transactions (money transfers, guarantees for agreements made with smugglers, loans). If the items sold were for the most part basic necessities (food and toiletries), also on offer were various items seen as deviant by the public authorities, either because they were subject to special regulation (tobacco and alcohol), or because they were suspected of being used for illegal crossings (such as the cutters used to tear the covers off lorries). This stigmatization was the reason why these businesses, the visible sign of the stabilization of the shantytown and its underground economy, would become the target of repressive action on the part of the authorities during the summer of 2016, prefiguring the demolition to come in October. However, as a sign of the normalization of everyday life in this space not recognized by the state, a delegation of traders from the Jungle visited the sub-prefecture to request authorization and tax registration. They did not win their case but managed to defer the destruction of restaurants by compliance with the fire regulations, before the government's appeal to the Conseil d'État allowed it to destroy them, starting on 18 October 2016. This demolition brought an end to the inextricable legal contradictions in which the stabilization of the shantytown had enmeshed the public authorities.

On the migrants' side, the differentiation of living conditions did create certain 'class' tensions. The traders shared the modest conditions of the other inhabitants. Yet on account of their income-generating activity, they formed a group rather less precarious than the others, and this position of relative notability brought with it certain obligations, for example to contribute towards the building of mosques, the funerals of people who died, or again to provide free meals for the poorest or most vulnerable members of the community.[6]

The poorest migrants, lacking any starting capital to open a shop, could still resort to another type of trade on the flea market held at night on the main street of the shantytown, where they would trade goods received from the voluntary organizations, in particular shoes and new clothes. In this way they could raise the few euros needed to buy cigarettes, or credit for their mobile phone. The destitute situation of the majority of the shantytown inhabitants also exposed them to forms of transaction that were not entirely consensual, to acquire the means of survival or the funds needed to pay for their crossing. The question of prostitution always arises, although information on this subject is very fragmentary. Studies have shown that not only were women affected by this phenomenon, but also men, particularly the youngest.[7]

The most lucrative activity for those engaged in it – and the most costly for its clients – was that bound up with the crossing to the UK. It is hard to define the word 'smuggler' ('*passeur*' in French), which can cover anyone from the bosses of mafia groups down to those individuals who occasionally share a good tip in exchange for remuneration, or again those who pay for the cost of their crossing by helping to close lorry doors or block the motorway. Yet it is around these activities that the largest sums of money circulated: €500 to access rest areas on the road where it was possible to hide in a lorry; up to €10,000 for a 'guaranteed' crossing with the complicity of a driver. This kind of assistance is subject to severe repression; the French authorities claim to have dismantled several 'networks' (around twenty in 2016) and arrested a large number of people involved in 'human trafficking' (over 600 in 2016) who face heavy penalties. Yet the intensification of border controls makes the role of smugglers increasingly indispensable. 'Independent' attempts by migrants to board the Channel Tunnel train, or hide in a lorry heading for the ferry, have relatively low success rates. In 2015, the border police discovered 38,000 migrants in lorries, and 49,000 in 2016.[8] So it is crossings with the complicity of the transporter (by road or sea) that make possible a successful crossing. The more sealed and controlled the border, the more the intermediaries can charge. Migrants unable to pay the cost of the crossing resort to 'chance', with ever more dangerous methods. For example, *douggars* are roadblocks erected on the motorway to create traffic jams; the migrants then try to climb into the lorries and hide, in the hope that amid the confusion some at least will sneak through police controls and detection systems, and reach the UK. Accidents are common, and sometimes fatal.

This activity linked to crossing attempts to England gave the everyday life of the shantytown a particular rhythm. Since the attempts were mostly at night, the day would begin late. Some migrants got up in the morning, particularly to reach the showers and the breakfast served at the Centre Jules Ferry, but social life scarcely got under way until around midday. Before this, the streets of the shantytown were full of various outsiders, volunteers and NGO staff going around to offer various services (legal, health, etc.), collect rubbish and organize distributions of food and clothing. At the end of the day, these outsiders would leave; the shantytown inhabitants prepared their meals, played football between the tents or cricket on the no man's land towards the CRS patrol at the camp entrance. As night fell, the streets were lively, with bars and clubs broadcasting music in an unlikely milieu of glitter balls, and small groups would leave the shantytown to try their luck on the motorway.

The atmosphere was very different depending on the time of day, the daylight hours being generally marked by a certain emptiness. A substantial part of the day was spent waiting in the 'lines' – queues at the distribution points for food, clothing or shower tickets. This waiting time was experienced as humiliating, placing the migrants in a position of passivity and subjugation. An apathetic daytime contrasted with the more active hours of night. Only a minority practised a professional activity in the Jungle (shopkeeper, cook, carpenter, etc.), and for the majority everyday life was marked by a certain idleness. Yet the waiting time was filled with a busy sociability, both among migrants themselves and with the volunteers who constituted an important resource for services and entertainment.

The large presence of volunteers and organizations made possible the development of a relatively diverse supply of activities during the day. Several schools were built, offering English and French lessons (the Darfour school, Jungle Books, the Chemin des Dunes school). Some people became real local figures (and international ones, through the media), such as Liz, a British woman who came to live in the shantytown, took care of unaccompanied minors and established an activities centre for women and children; or Zimako, a Nigerian migrant who came from Nice to support the inhabitants of the Calais shantytown and initiated the Chemin des Dunes school. Several artistic projects were started, from the 'Arts and Crafts School' set up by Alpha, a Mauritian migrant and artist who soon became a celebrity in the camp, to the one-off projects of Art in the Jungle and the various workshops conducted for children. The voluntary organizations also supported sports activities by providing equipment for football, volleyball and cricket. Only a few migrants went into the town daily, although the French Catholic Relief/ Caritas and Calais Migrant Solidarity offered French classes there, thus opening up a bit this shantytown ghetto wedged between the industrial zone and the sea.

Religion held a major place among the activities, giving rhythm and structure to social life. There were several places of worship, some of these dating back to the establishment of the shantytown in spring 2015, such as the Eritrean Orthodox church, while others (Methodist, Islamic) were built by various communities as they arrived. All of these provided a spiritual support that helped the refugees cope with the psychological suffering and multiple traumas that afflicted them. Religion cemented social relations in a specific community, especially for minority religions such as Orthodox Christians or Shia. But the place of worship could also be a space for mingling between communities, as was the case with the large Sunni 'Omar' mosque, where several communities converged for prayer on Fridays and religious celebrations. The imam was also able to play the part of mediator and reconciler, pacifying relations that were sometimes tense – particularly between Afghans and Sudanese. Religion thus appeared as a regulator of social life, appealed to for establishing rules in a space perceived as offering little security.

The fragility of the social fabric of the Jungle was made palpable by the importance of rumours. The Jungle was a space where people were very familiar with one another, even though the mobile population was constantly bringing new faces. This particular configuration, in a context of great precariousness and uncertainty, was propitious for rumours – unverified news exchanged in contexts of interaction within which it acquired a meaning beyond its actual content. For example, rumours about a member of another community could serve both to stigmatize it and at the same time weld cohesion within one's own community, regardless of the truth or falsity of the information. Rumour could express regular modalities of sociability, but also be a response to a critical situation, a symptom of social disorder. By their diversity and profusion, rumours circulating in the Calais Jungle were symptoms of the intensity of social relations, as well as the agonizing situation of uncertainty in which the migrants lived. In such a society, unstable and shifting, uncertainty bore most of all on individual identity. For example, a Sudanese man told how one of his compatriots recently killed by an Afghan in a brawl by the ring road leading to the port was an informer for the Sudanese government: 'So why was he killed? Because he came to cause trouble in the Jungle, perhaps so that the French government will close it. He wanted to sully the reputation of the Sudanese.'

Some rumours amounted to political commentary, on the risks that refugees experienced or their present perspectives. In June 2016, for example, three months after the demolition of the southern zone of the shantytown, speculation was rife about a possible demolition of the northern zone. At the same time, the vote in the UK on the Brexit referendum gave rise to several rumours: Britain was going to refuse all refugees; France was going to break the Le Touquet agreements and let everyone cross to Britain; Nicolas Sarkozy (then candidate in the right-wing primaries for the 2017 presidential election) would force the British to open the border. These rumours expressed more or less well-informed appropriations of the political context (Sarkozy had asserted a strong position on border control; he wanted to close the Calais shantytown as he had closed Sangatte in 2002). The sharing of more or less accurate news fuelled conversations, enabled points of view to be compared, and offered interpretations in a situation of great geopolitical uncertainty.

Other types of rumour reflected fears and anxieties, particularly around death, violence and moral laxity – particularly in the form of lechery. Recurrent rumours spread around the Jungle about the 'real' number of migrant deaths at Calais, several of whom were supposedly concealed and the bodies buried in the dunes. From the direction of the town, too, rumours of violence in relation to the Jungle were just as common, concerning the number of assaults, rapes and murders that the authorities supposedly concealed, with the complicity of the media. Some of these rumours emanated directly from the police unions, who did not flinch from using them to demand a higher budget.[9] The rumours about rapes were particularly recurrent, attesting to the very real worries about a threat that groups of foreign young men might cause. Conversely, however, recurrent rumours in the Jungle told of sexual deviance, sometimes parallel to those disturbing the Calais population. Ahmed, a 25-year-old Afghan, told of a prostitution case centring on a young boy from Calais,

> still a kid, he often comes and does stuff with men in the huts, so much so that they stand outside in a line, and the noise

disturbs prayer in the mosque! The whole Jungle knows about it, it's not hidden at all! Men wait their turn just like at the food distributions! And that creates fights, for example the other day one Afghan tried to stop another Afghan entering the hut, saying that it was immoral, and the other replied 'This is Europe, I'll do what I want'. They fought, it was a real scandal – and just outside the mosque!

Ahmed wanted to denounce this boy to the police, to have him arrested for prostitution, he said. In this rumour that he related (the content of which was never verified), the agent of moral corruption was not the migrant but the local young-ster whose disrupting behaviour related to the worries and uncertainties of migration.

Making a community

The shantytown was a particular social space, where no legitimate authority intervened to ensure respect for the laws generally applicable on French territory, or provide public ser-vices that are usually free. The police – who strictly patrolled the access points to cross-border transport and sometimes brutally repressed attempts at intrusion (violent arrests, tear gas sprayed around the ring road leading to the port and even in the shantytown dwellings) – only rarely entered the encampment. Operations did take place in the context of the investigation of people-smuggling rings, or following decisions by the prefecture about businesses or the eviction of specific areas. Yet despite repeated requests from some shantytown inhabitants, no regular police patrol followed and the emergency services did not respond to calls, fuelling among some people the sense of living in a lawless zone, where the safety of people and their belongings could not be ensured. However, the absence of public authorities was partly made up for by the commitment of the NGOs, vol-untary organizations and individuals who provided a wide range of services, from first aid and putting out of fires through to mediation to resolve interpersonal conflicts.

The need for civil life made itself felt, in debates over how diverse migrant communities could coexist and how charities were to help them. This gave rise to an institution specific to the place: 'community leaders' who represented their respective communities (Afghan, Sudanese, Eritrean, Kurdish, Egyptian, Syrian, Ethiopian, etc.) vis-à-vis both aid organizations and the public authorities. These 'community leaders' were partly created by the need of the voluntary organizations to identify spokespeople, in order to circulate information and negotiate decisions. They were individuals who had been at Calais for a long time, and whose legitimacy was largely based on their identification by the organizations as intermediaries for their community. They might thus find themselves in the position of redistributors of goods and services, which enabled them to gain some authority over other refugees. They would be questioned as spokespeople for their community on the occasion of weekly meetings with the organizations active on the site, as well as at meetings with the public authorities – sub-prefect or police superintendent – who involved them as mediators to pacify relations between migrant communities and facilitate their compliance with decisions of the authorities that affected them. This was particularly the case in spring 2015, when the various squats and encampments in the town had to be abandoned in favour of the encampment on the 'lande'. Likewise, in autumn 2016, with the evacuation of the Jungle for the Temporary Accommodation Centres opened in different places across France.

Political expression was not confined to these community leaders, whose legitimacy was not recognized by everyone. The various decisions collectively affecting the inhabitants of the shantytown, such as the eviction from the southern zone announced in February 2016, were occasions of political socialization and mobilization, employing a variety of types of action, including demonstrations, court appearances and hunger strike. These modalities of resistance and expression of demands could have been affected by political experiences in the country of origin or during migration, or again by encounters with volunteers able to instruct migrants about the legal means of making their claims vis-à-vis the authorities. For example, a hundred or so migrants living in the shantytown appealed to the administrative tribunal against the demolition of the southern zone of the shantytown in February 2016, though they obtained satisfaction only on the preservation of collective spaces such as places of worship, schools, and other constructions that provided health care

Photo 8. The Calais Jungle, October 2016 (photo: Sara Prestianni).

or legal information. While upholding the prefecture's decision to halt the expansion of the shantytown, the tribunal recognized that this was not just a makeshift camp but had become an effective community.

Despite being on the edge of an urban centre, built with makeshift materials and the help of volunteers and associations, as the months passed the Calais Jungle became stabilized in its precariousness. Coexistence between communities was not established without clashes, but it made possible, none the less, the formation of a kind of experimental society made up of very heterogeneous groups, forced to live together in the same space on account of the provision of services there, and the repression of unlawful camps elsewhere. Their relationship to the place was ambivalent, uncomfortable and violent, the shantytown was at the same time a reassuring cocoon, a place of solidarities, where the cost of access to services was very low on account of the presence of other refugees, and of volunteers able to act as intermediaries, offering guidance and explaining procedures. In the course of 2016, the Calais Jungle thus became a focal point for migrants, whether or not they wanted to reach the UK (see photo 8).

4

A Jungle of solidarities

Calais, and more broadly the migrant encampments in northern France, became – as if echoing the media theme of a 'European refugee crisis' – places of strong mobilization of citizens for solidarity, on a local, national and international scale. This solidarity had new characteristics in relation to that developed in the previous fifteen years in the Calais region. Whereas the earlier period had been marked by the creation of several local *associations*,[1] a strong internationalization then followed, expressed in the increased presence of major humanitarian NGOs and a marked involvement of individuals who decided to share the daily life of migrants for months at a time.

Calais as a cosmopolitan crossroads of solidarities

The excitement of the Calais Jungle was a striking experience. Each weekend, hundreds of volunteers and activists[2] converged, working to distribute meals and clothing, run artistic workshops or offer legal advice. Intended to make up for the inadequacy of the public authorities, this solidarity also developed as an alternative experiment, occupying the space of the shantytown as a place to develop or even inhabit.

During the summer of 2016, around forty groups of various status were active on the Calais site, offering a wide range of services and activities, either permanent or one-off, run either by volunteers or professionals.

The authorities set up reception services for the Calais migrants only belatedly and inadequately, since they never wanted to officially recognize this shantytown, created 'by accident' following a decision aimed at expelling the informal squats and encampments in the town centre. Forms of institutional solidarity were extended by professional bodies under contract from the state. This was the case with the Centre Jules Ferry, opened in January 2015 by La Vie Active, which distributed hot meals, offered showers, and provided a shelter for women and children. Likewise, the Centre d'Accueil Provisoire, opened in January 2016, also run by La Vie Active. Finally, there were services of water provision, cleaning and roadways provided under contract by the NGO ACTED, following a legal case brought against the failures of the state in November 2015. La Vie Active is an organization specializing in social housing (for old people, minors and the homeless), well established in the Nord department but with no speciality in migrant questions. Among its hundred or so employees, it recruited many people from the medico-social sector, as well as volunteers working with migrants and some recent migrants themselves. Its close connection with the authorities, however, cut it off from the milieu of local voluntary organizations, and its relations with these were either tense or non-existent. However, many volunteers participated in its activities. As for ACTED, this had a particular mandate, as it became the official manager of an illegal site, on which it had neither the power nor the desire to exercise control. As a result, apart from maintenance tasks, it sought rather to coordinate the joint management of the site by migrant communities, voluntary organizations and individuals, holding gatherings and operational meetings. ACTED, being an international NGO with a speciality in crisis intervention (post-conflict or post-catastrophe), was involved in France for the first time, part of the phenomenon of internationalization of the Calais question in the course of 2015.

The Calais Jungle became a cosmopolitan crossroads of civil solidarity efforts. Though it is hard to quantify the international involvement, it was clearly apparent in the contingents of the two organizations that mobilized the largest number of volunteers, Care4Calais and Auberge des Migrants/Help Refugees. Auberge des Migrants, which up to 2015 had counted only around twenty volunteers, often younger retired people from Calais, underwent a lightning growth with the influx of several hundred young British volunteers during summer 2015, thanks in part to its alliance with Help Refugees, an organization established ad hoc to help the Calais migrants. These organizations played a key role in the everyday survival of thousands of shantytown inhabitants, to whom they distributed ready-made meals, foodstuffs, clothing, tents, covers, etc., mobilizing logistic resources that were considerable for non-professional bodies. The actions undertaken by these organizations transformed the local solidarity landscape at Calais, both by the scale of the human and financial means mobilized, and by ways of acting that were more iconoclastic and more professional in terms of communication and organization of activity. The annual operating budget of Auberge des Migrants rose from around €100,000 in 2014 (including €20,000 in public grants) to €944,000 in 2015 (of which only €5,000 was in public grants). This considerable increase in financial resources was combined with a still more remarkable growth in human resources, with an average of 120 volunteers per day in 2016 active in the warehouse on behalf of the Auberge des Migrants, Help Refugees, and other partner organizations such as Refugee Community Kitchen.

The outreach and central position that Auberge des Migrants acquired in this context makes it useful to focus on this particular case and give something of its history. It began in 2003 with the foundation of Salam,[3] which grew out of the C'SUR collective.[4] Salam gave humanitarian aid to migrants, as well as supporting members of voluntary organizations prosecuted for solidarity work. In 2008, internal disagreements led to a split and the creation of Auberge des Migrants, starting with a small group of volunteers in a context of sharp tension with the public authorities and division over the proper place of voluntary organizations.[5] The Auberge focused on the distribution of meals and clothing.

From summer 2015, it would undergo an exponential transformation and become a flagship organization, as an 'umbrella' for several others. Capitalizing on the high demand for volunteers, it linked up with Help Refugees, an organization formed by young British people, with experience in running events and a great capacity for mobilization. Auberge des Migrants received a deluge of donations and rented a hangar that became a major logistics hub, while a substantial volunteer staff built up. There were always at least a dozen volunteers at work, and up to 200 during the vacations. Seventy per cent were women, and despite the presence of French people, the majority were British (largely from southern England), as well as many Irish. Activities consisted in the preparation of meals (Calais Kitchen provided 2,000 meals per day for Calais and Grande-Synthe), packs of foodstuffs, the sorting of clothes and tents for distribution, the construction of huts and other items such as stoves for heating. On the actual site, the Auberge set up the Welcome Caravan to receive newcomers, give them a starting kit and help them find a place to stay in the Jungle.

Two different emphases can be distinguished within the organization, particularly according to nationality. While the majority of people working in the hangar were British (and other nationalities, for example Belgian, German, Dutch and American, etc.), organizing practical support in the way of sorting and large-scale distribution, the historical pillars of the organization were supported by French trainees (and from September 2016 'civic services'), who managed connections with other organizations and set up one-off projects (for example, the enrolment of eighty students from the Jungle at the Université de Lille).

The Auberge des Migrants also became one of the main actors in establishing general policies for the voluntary organizations. It was a major distribution centre for assistance of all kinds. Some of the organization's volunteers did not flinch from adopting an expression used to refer to them: a 'humanitarian machine'.

Because the Auberge des Migrants, together with Help Refugees, had such large resources in the way of 'labour power', these organizations were able to carry out headcounts of the Jungle residents, and played a major role with

the media and the public authorities. They were consulted by
the prefecture in October 2016, when this envisaged demol-
ishing the shantytown and transferring its inhabitants to
'reception and orientation' centres.

Many other organizations and individual volunteers
involved themselves in the life of the Calais shantytown either
daily or sporadically, offering various services. There were,
for example, several communal kitchens established on the
site: Belgium Kitchen, which gave out 1,000 meals per day,
and Ashram Kitchen, which distributed 500 meals per day.
Kitchen in Calais was originally set up by a Malaysian family
who had settled in the UK. Moved by the fate of refugees
in Calais, they decided to go there in September 2015 and
distribute aid. Realizing the scale of need in terms of hot
meals, the family decided to install a caravan and cook on
site. Their initiative received wide support, particularly from
generous British donors, so that the kitchen expanded and by
2016 was able to distribute over 1,500 meals each day. Large
donations came from Islamic solidarity networks in Britain,
France (Lille and Paris regions), and sometimes from more
distant countries (Turkey, Dubai).

The Refugee Community Kitchen, for its part, was the
initiative of a punk festival organizer, who joined up with
the Auberge des Migrants and set up an 'industrial' kitchen
to prepare up to 2,500 daily meals using fresh produce,
for Calais and Grande-Synthe. 'Community kitchen leaders'
acted on each site to assist the communal kitchens. With
the support of Help Refugees and Auberge des Migrants,
the Refugee Community Kitchen claims to have prepared
more than half a million meals between December 2015 and
September 2016. It also benefited from substantial volunteer
networks in artistic milieus, and possessed a great capacity
for media mobilization, along with chefs who came to lend
a hand. The organizations estimated the number of their
volunteers at some 7,500 over the course of a year.

Several distribution points were also established, such as
the containers of Care4Calais or the Welcome Caravan of
the Auberge des Migrants, offering what new arrivals immediately needed (tents, blankets, hygiene kits). Organizations
such as the French Utopia 56 (more involved at Grande-
Synthe in the early days of the humanitarian camp of La

Linière) and the British Greenlight set out to collect rubbish, as did ACTED agents on behalf of the state; each of these mobilized several dozen volunteers.

On the health side, the French NGO Médecins du Monde, which had worked with migrant populations in northern France since 2005, through its mission Migrants Littoral Nord-Pas-de-Calais, opened a clinic in September 2015, which was then taken over by the Calais hospital (Permanence d'Accès aux Soins). Médecins Sans Frontières focused on mental health and support for unaccompanied minors (in May 2016, a day centre for minors was opened in the shantytown). Gynécologie Sans Frontières offered services to migrant women. British volunteers set up several 'First Aid Caravans', as well as a vaccination centre, a temporary dentist's office, and a dispensary established by Humming Bird (a local initiative of Brighton residents). Elise Care offered acupuncture services, which enjoyed great success with the migrants, with several thousand consultations.

In terms of legal support, information on asylum in France was provided by agents of the government asylum services and their immigration counterpart from offices in the Centre Jules Ferry and the CAP, or else in Calais town from the associations Secours Catholique and France Terre d'Asile – the latter entrusted with this mission by the state. In the shantytown itself, however, there was little in the way of legal services. Calais Migrant Solidarity and the No Border movement gave out legal information leaflets from 'Info Points' in the Jungle. From September 2015, two French lawyers worked for unaccompanied minors with families in the UK, who therefore had legal ways of crossing the border. Citizen UK, through its Safe Passage programme, sent teams of British lawyers, from autumn 2015 onwards, to establish cases in support of these unaccompanied minors. It was not until spring 2016 that a mission of France Terre d'Asile was contracted by the state to deal with these cases. Legal information and access to courts, for minors as well as for all migrants faced with the many problems bound up with their plans (asylum application in France, family reunion) or their experience of repression (police violence), were basically provided on the site by a small volunteer structure, set up in the context of the Appel de Calais (also known as the Appel des 800), the Cabane Juridique/Legal Shelter. From summer 2016, the Refugee Info Bus also supplied information on asylum in the UK.

Apart from these food, health and legal services, individuals and voluntary organizations working with the migrants also offered a wide variety of sociocultural activities, as mentioned in chapter 3, illustrating the significant place of these initiatives in the everyday social life of the Jungle inhabitants. Thus, 'schools' grew up around volunteers offering classes in French or English: the École du Darfour, the École Laïque du Chemin des Dunes, Jungle Books, etc. These offered classes for both children and adults. And in June 2016, the state school system opened a class for children of compulsory school age at the CAP. Artistic activities, workshops in citizen journalism and games were also offered. The Good Chance Theatre, established by two young British playwrights, organized improvisation workshops, concerts, film shows, and theatrical performances by some of the most famous British companies from October 2015 to March 2016, thanks to the exceptional financing it received. The Women Centre offered activities particularly designed for women and children, while the Baloo Centre and the Kids' Restaurant offered other activities for adolescents.

These various forms of support contributed to shaping the space of the Jungle, establishing services to make up for the insufficient contribution of the French state, which did not recognize the encampment as a 'refugee' camp, and refused to accept its de facto permanence. Support also came for the material improvement of the site, in the form of earth-moving equipment and construction materials. Solidarity from citizens thus directly contributed to the urbanization of the site. Both ACTED and the Auberge des Migrants cleared and flattened spaces, and drained certain flooded zones. A number of organizations and volunteers brought tents, caravans, huts in kit form, yurts, etc. For example, the French punk network Boule Eud'Pue built around 200 dwellings at a cost of €400 each in terms of materials, or a total of €80,000; Secours Catholique estimates to have spent €30,000 on materials for huts, and Médecins Sans Frontières €720,000 for over a thousand shelters; Auberge des Migrants and Help Refugees together more than €400,000 for about 1,500 shelters. Several individuals brought tents, caravans, and some yurts. The British organizations Caravans for Calais and Jungle Canopy were allowed to bring mobile homes to house migrants or activities designed for them. Charpentiers Sans Frontières constructed the building that housed the Cabane Juridique. A countless number of 'good-willed' individuals brought camping tents, sometimes military tents or other materials to give shelter from the inclement weather of the northern French coast, also to build a kind of urban utopia, experimenting with forms of collective habitat and equipment on a site that largely escaped the control of the state in its internal organization, as we have seen in chapter 2. For its part, in fact, the state's intervention in the shanty-town was essentially negative, in the form of constraint and restriction, for example by limiting the space that could be used or banning the entry of building materials.

A certain 'experimentation' also took place on the level of human relations, with volunteers settling in the Jungle in order to share the everyday life of the refugees. This was not a strictly novel practice, as the mode of operation of the No Border movement, for example, is to reject the demarcation between migrants and their supporters, particularly by inhabiting squats themselves. In 2015, however, with the settlement of the Jungle de la Lande, this mode of intervention acquired an unequalled scale. At times, several dozen supporters lived on the site for longer or shorter periods. These played a major role in access to various services (for example, taking people to hospital), allocating resources (identifying the 'vulnerable'), regulating relationships and resolving conflicts, etc. Their intervention and their choice of life was not always understood by the migrants, who were forced to tolerate unhealthy conditions that they had certainly not chosen. The fact that the majority of these supporters were young single women, in an environment made up chiefly of young single men, was seen by the migrants as the most common explanation, each side having an interest in the arrangement. The formation of couples would reinforce this interpretation. Moreover, this presence was perceived as subversive by the public authorities, who tended to equate it with the No Border movement, reputedly 'radical' and 'violent'. The motives for settling in the Jungle could be diverse, however, from total commitment, through simply continuing a marginal trajectory, to a desire for an unusual experience. This 'encampment' of volunteers also led to promoting alternative approaches to aid that were more attentive to cultural differences, to individual sensitivities, and finally to the words of migrants themselves.

This attention was formalized in 'community meetings' held each week, in the course of which representatives of the main communities present in the shantytown (Afghans, Sudanese, Kurds, Eritreans, Ethiopians, Syrians, Egyptians, Iranians) discussed the ways in which the people supporting them intervened in relation to their various needs. Food and clothing distribution was the object of endless debate, given both its importance for the migrants and the power it gave those controlling these resources. But the personal conduct of the volunteers also came under discussion, and in spring 2016 a 'code of conduct' was drawn up, to ensure 'mutual respect': volunteers were requested not to take photos, to be attentive to cultural particularities, and not to drink alcohol in public. This code of conduct, however, enjoyed only limited adherence, given the reluctance of the voluntary organizations to impose rules of behaviour on their participants without reciprocity on the part of the migrants. It did, however, express the significant 'encampment' of solidarity activity within the Calais shantytown, i.e. the fact that certain volunteers chose to settle in the place, making regulation necessary from the point of view of the migrants who were there under constraint.

A further rationale of this code of conduct, which was drawn up by the weekly community meeting of the migrants, was the scale acquired by a form of humanitarian tourism, solidarity in the form of a one-off visit, enabling people to take in the situation there, to be moved by it, to satisfy a certain curiosity or even a certain desire for exoticism. Visitors were very numerous in 2015 and 2016, some coming to lend a hand for a day or two, others to research,[6] film or photograph for a journalistic report, an artistic project, or simply a souvenir.

These new forms of support tended to eclipse the local network of the volunteers and collectives, which was largely overtaken by the situation in 2015, when the number of migrants grew substantially and the interventions of the public authorities caused substantial divisions. The association

Salam, established in 2003 after the closure of the Sangatte camp and a pillar of daily support for the migrants for more than ten years, distributing hot meals and clothing, began to decline after the loss of its premises and the opening of the Jules Ferry day centre – which was generally called 'Salam' by the migrants, despite being run by La Vie Active under contract from the state. Secours Catholique also found itself overtaken by the situation, despite its strong local anchorage bound up with a large network of volunteers. In autumn 2015 it launched a legal action against the state to demand better facilities for the migrants, relegated to a shantytown without any basic services. However, it remained a partner recognized by the public authorities, particularly in autumn 2016 when it came to negotiating the expulsion from the shantytown in favour of the Centres d'Accueil et d'Orientation.

New organizations would reconfigure the local solidarity landscape, marked by recurring (and shifting) divisions between 'humanitarians' and 'activists'. Whereas the humanitarian pole was represented by organizations such as Salam or the Auberge des Migrants, the activist and more protesting pole was represented by Calais Migrant Solidarity, which arose from the No Border camp of 2009 and whose purpose was to combine support for migrants with political mobilization for the opening of borders. This protesting pole was made up of a wide spread of profiles, a common point for whom was defiance towards the public authorities and recourse to illegal methods to make up for the inadequacies of reception, with the opening of squats such as the Victor Hugo squat in Calais town for the reception of women and children (this would be taken over by the state in 2014, its inhabitants subsequently transferred to the Centre Jules Ferry). Another common point for all these organizations was denunciation of the repression against the migrants, with demonstrations against the administrative detention centres and the documentation of police violence.

The situation in other encampments

The town of Calais and its closest surroundings saw not only the concentration of the highest number of migrants in the north of France, but also the greatest number of solidarity actions in support of them, and the greatest media and political interest in this subject. During the 1990s, encampments were gradually established in smaller municipalities along the motorways leading to Calais. In the wake of the presence of migrants, forms of solidarity also developed across the region, initially in the form of individual initiatives, then with the gradual formation of more formal collectives and associations (as provided for by the law of 1901). Between 2008 and 2011, several voluntary organizations were established, for example Terre d'Errance at Steenvoorde and Norrent-Fontes, Flandre Terre Solidaire at Bailleul, the Collectif Fraternité Migrants Bassin Minier 62 at Angres, Terre d'Errance Flandre Littoral at Bollezeele, and Aide Migrants Solidarité at Téteghem.

Around the migrant encampments, whose occupants ranged from a few dozen individuals to several hundred, forms of solidarity were chiefly the act of individual well-wishers and local voluntary organizations. Civic solidarity thus developed in a space relatively ignored by the major humanitarian organizations, after the interlude of the reception centre at Sangatte run by the Red Cross. These local initiatives did not receive grants; they collected donations in the form of food and clothing, as well as funds raised by membership subscriptions or public events such as concerts or exhibitions.

The Norrent-Fontes encampment and Terre d'Errance

This was, for example, the case at Norrent-Fontes, where the first migrants arrived in the late 1990s. This municipality is situated in the department of Pas-de-Calais, between Lillers and Aire-sur-la-Lys, a rural area about 75 kilometres from the town of Calais. Though Norrent-Fontes is not a coastal town, it can be seen as a 'border town', being close to the A26 motorway, known as the 'Autoroute des Anglais', which connects Paris and Calais. More precisely, it was the existence of a service station on the territory of the adjacent municipality of Saint-Hilaire-Cottes that explained the presence of migrants. For car and lorry drivers coming from

Paris, this was the last rest stop before reaching Calais that had a filling station, a restaurant, toilets and showers. Lorry drivers frequently paused for a break here, offering an opportunity for migrants to try each night to climb into the lorries stationed in the parking bays. To reach this service station and the lorries parked there, the migrants had about 1,500 metres from the encampment where they lived, taking paths that were often muddy and arousing complaints from the neighbouring farmers.

Far from the political and media farrago that Calais experienced, the municipality of Norrent-Fontes seemed far more peaceful. According to the last census, it had 1,500 permanent residents, in addition to whom were the 200-odd migrants living in the encampment. About half of these were women. This high proportion was a particularity of the Norrent-Fontes encampment in relation to other sites in the region occupied by migrants (particularly the towns of Calais and Grande-Synthe). At Norrent-Fontes, there was little sign of the migrants during the daytime. Apart from the church, the migrants only visited a few shops: the baker's, the café, the service station, and a local farm products outlet where they occasionally bought milk and yoghurt. The rest of their shopping was most often done at a discount supermarket in the next village.

The encampment where the migrants lived at Norrent-Fontes was at the end of the Rue de Rely, about 2 kilometres from the main road through the village. A clump of trees concealed a few wooden huts and tents, where some migrants had lived for several months. In 2012, four wooden huts were constructed on some public land between the fields that was not used by the municipality. The mayor at the time, a member of Europe-Écologie/Les Verts and president of the Réseau des Élus Hospitaliers [Network of Hospitable Elected Officials], had supported this initiative. In April 2015, following an accidental fire caused by an oil lamp, two of these huts were destroyed. A few months later, activists worked on the reconstruction of a building to shelter the occupants of the camp. During this year the number of migrants grew, and tents were gradually erected a bit further away, on unused private farmland. It was mainly men who lived here. The three huts still standing were used for cooking, storage of foodstuffs, and accommodation for women. The encampment had neither water nor electricity. At its centre was an old caravan used as a sick bay and medical office attended by a GP and two nurses, all volunteers. Once a week, volunteers drove groups of migrants to take a shower in the changing rooms of the sports facilities in neighbouring municipalities (see photo 9).

At the end of the 1990s, the support given to migrant populations in the municipality of Norrent-Fontes was initially expressed in private and one-off initiatives on the part of local residents, connected by networks of family, friendship and religious community. These forms of support were gradually organized, leading to the creation in 2008 of Terre d'Errance, which until recently was the only group active in the migrant camp in this municipality. It was exclusively made up of volunteers, counting in 2016 around forty activists and nearly 500 members. Financial and material resources came from subscriptions, private donations, and food products or construction materials that were collected.

The greater part of the organization's activities consisted in emergency support: access to drinking water, health care and hygiene (toilets and showers), the construction of makeshift shelters, distribution of food, clothing, footwear and

Photo 9. The Norrent-Fontes encampment, 2016 (photo: Julien Saison).

blankets. While this humanitarian activity structured the activists' everyday life, the members of Terre d'Errance also undertook actions to raise awareness among the local population, particularly in schools. On these visits, volunteers informed students about the origin of the refugee populations, why they had arrived in France, and what their living conditions were. Terre d'Errance also took part, along with other local and national organizations, in informing and questioning citizens, elected representatives and other political agents.

Although some of these volunteers visited Calais from time to time, for example to take part in demonstrations, picketing or meetings with other organizations, collective events were also arranged occasionally in the encampment at Norrent-Fontes. Following the fire that destroyed some of the huts, volunteers began the construction of a new shelter in 2015. On this occasion, the new mayor of Norrent-Fontes, who had been elected the previous year, issued a municipal order banning any rebuilding on this site. Several Terre d'Errance activists were then interviewed in the context of an investigation by the national gendarmerie. As a reaction to this, a day of mobilization was organized at the encampment on 10 October 2015, under the slogan 'Building hospitality'. Several volunteers worked to complete the construction of the new shelter, and concerts were organized throughout the day in the presence of several local and national organizations that had come to lend support. Nearly a year later, on 14 September 2016, a day of mobilization, this time called 'Fields of resistance', was organized to protest against the demolition of the encampment that had been demanded by the mayor and the private owners of land occupied by the shelters and tents of the migrants. And another year later, on 18 September 2017, the encampment of Norrent-Fontes was entirely evacuated and destroyed by the police.

The 'humanitarian camp' at Grande-Synthe: local and European solidarity

Another coastal encampment found itself in the spotlight in winter 2015–16. This was the encampment at Grande-Synthe, close to the port of Dunkirk. Established some ten years earlier in a wood in a residential zone, known as Le Basroch, the encampment, whose occupants were mainly Kurds, experienced a sharp rise in its population from 2014. From around 300 at that time, it grew by December 2015 to more than 2,500 persons, including many women and children. Médecins du Monde had been active there for a long time, as had local collectives of volunteers. In the autumn, volunteers from Britain and other European countries arrived to bring support, some of whom settled on the site.

Faced with the critical situation at the end of 2015, the Ecologist mayor of the town, a member of the Réseau des Élus Hospitaliers, called on the state to provide shelter for the encampment's inhabitants. Failing to obtain satisfaction, he decided to call on Médecins Sans Frontières to build a 'camp to humanitarian norms' in order to keep migrants out of the mud. A site close to the motorway was made available by the town hall, close to the premises of a former agricultural cooperative, La Linière. The camp was built by MSF at its own expense, for a sum of €2.6 million. It consisted of 380 wooden shelters designed to accommodate four people each. Toilet blocks were installed, as well as communal kitchens and buildings for social and cultural activity.

The town hall initially earmarked €500,000 towards the operation of the site, though its everyday expenses would basically rely on private initiatives. Utopia 56 saw to logistics and the everyday coordination of all volunteers when the site was opened in March 2016. At that time about a thousand people were housed here. Utopia 56 is a voluntary organization without an activist past or local anchorage. It originated at Lorient in Brittany, on the initiative of temporary workers at seasonal festivals (for example, the Festival des Vieilles Charrues), who discovered the situation at Calais during winter 2015–16.[7] Initially involved with the Auberge des Migrants and the collection of refuse from the Calais shantytown, Utopia 56 then focused principally on Grande-Synthe. Between February and September 2016, some 3,000 volunteers worked at the site for a total of more than 17,000 days.

On top of this, some fifty other organizations gave support, both local (Emmaüs Dunkerque, Salam, etc.) and international. Thus, while no public financing was envisaged for food aid, the Refugee Community Kitchen (run by British volunteers) and Kisha Neya (founded by German volunteers) ensured food daily thanks to donations and voluntary work.

The government rejected on principle the establishment of a refugee camp at Grande-Synthe, but faced with a fait accompli, it finally agreed to finance the management of the site in April 2016, contracting this to a professional body, the AFEJI.[8] When the Calais Jungle was demolished in October 2016, the population of the Grande-Synthe camp rose to 1,000 individuals (and to 1,700 by March 2017), but a stricter control on entry (with identification by bracelet) enabled this increase to be contained. So as not to make the humanitarian camp permanent, the town hall demanded a reduction in its capacity, and the cabins were dismantled as their occupants left. Living conditions deteriorated, and the aid organizations denounced an increase in violence, particularly towards women and unaccompanied minors. Added to this was the exasperation of migrants unable to pass the border controls, who made increasingly dangerous attempts to intercept lorries heading for the UK, particularly by blocking the motorway. On 10 April 2017, violent brawls between certain groups of migrants led to a fire at the camp that almost completely destroyed it. After the closure of the camp, the migrants roamed around and set up precarious encampments in woods, from which they were often expelled by the police.

Mobilization networks: from local to national

The experience of solidarity at Calais and other encampments on the northern coast of France makes it possible to sketch out a typology: local activists and volunteers; NGOs and professional associations; new actors in refugee aid who straddle the border between voluntary commitment and professionalism. Whereas local solidarity until 2015 depended largely on retired people, mobilized through political, trade union or religious networks, the profile of the new supporters was more varied: often younger (a large number of students), without previous activist experience, and mobilized by affinity group or by particular geographical factors (Kent, Sussex, Dublin, Ghent).

Local networks of migrant support

The local network of activists and volunteers was made up of people who were often retired and with a varied activist background, stretching from the Catholic left through trade unionists to former 'Maoists', or else from religious denominations. This network was regional rather than strictly local. The engagement of left-wing activists fitted into their historical commitment in favour of Algerian independence, the strikes of 1968, support for the workers of the Lip factory, the movement to defend Larzac, as well as the hunger strikes of undocumented immigrants. These activists were often also members of other organizations, from the Parti Communiste Français to the trade unions, and for the 'left Catholics', organizations such as ATD Quart Monde. This commitment also fitted into a Christian morality of welcome and hospitality, expressed through La Pastorale des Migrants or the network of volunteers and 'harbourers' of Secours Catholique and parishes across the region. Islamic solidarity networks were also organized, chiefly from working-class districts in the Lille area. One example of this was Oumma Fourchette based at Roubaix, which had worked alongside Salam at Calais since 2003 in preparing meals, and from 2015 carried out a weekly delivery of foodstuffs as well as help to Islamic migrants in the construction of mosques in the Calais shantytown and assistance with funerals in the case of deaths. Other groups had a similar recruitment pattern in working-class districts with a large immigrant population, without necessarily situating their initiative in a religious context, such as the Association Lutter pour L'Égalité, contre la discrimination et pour la solidarité, particularly based at Lille and Courrière, which organized food distributions at Calais and other encampments in the north of France.

The diversity of trajectories of commitment to migrants was also a source of divisions, which shifted and recomposed with the evolution of government policy and the attitude of the public authorities towards the supporters of migrants.

The year 2009 marked a turning point, with the No Border camp organized during the summer, which attracted groups from across Europe that had formed in support of foreigners. An alter-globalist movement formed in 1999 to challenge European policies of migration control, No Border proposed an ideological reading of the border as an instrument of capitalist domination, and demanded freedom of movement and settlement for all. Without formal membership, and a relatively flexible structure, this movement was viewed with suspicion by the authorities, who suspected it of organizing illegal activities, manipulating migrants and being responsible for the human overflow. The intervention of the No Border movement at Calais, followed by that of Calais Migrant Solidarity, shifted the landscape of local solidarity towards a more protesting activism, as well as one more internationalized.

The question of a more 'humanitarian' stance as against a more 'political' one was an old one for migrant supporters, and perhaps still more so at Calais than elsewhere, given not only the particular acuteness of the humanitarian crisis, but also the repression of solidarity activity, and the virulence of xenophobic positions, including acts of violence and intimidation towards migrants and those helping them. Some people then maintained that the emergency was just as critical in the realm of ideas and focused their activity in this domain: this was the case with the Marmite aux Idées, the blog Passeurs d'hospitalité[9] and the group Calais, Ouverture et Humanité.[10]

NGOs and 'professional associations'

2015 marked a new turning point with the arrival of the major NGOs on the scene. This intervention was on unaccustomed ground, given that they were more familiar with the migrants' countries of origin. The Syrian drama, the drownings in the Mediterranean, and the inability of the European authorities to protect refugees, led these international NGOs to focus on this 'emergency' and formulate proposals for intervention. Professionals of international humanitarian aid then arrived at the encampments in northern France, after careers in the refugee camps of Congo, Syria, in medical dispensaries in Afghanistan or displaced persons camps in Haiti. At Calais, the major international NGOs such as Médecins Sans Frontières applied the pattern they had used abroad: the assumption of a deficient state with which it was necessary to enter into diplomatic negotiations; the specialization of functions by 'mission' (management, operations, communications, etc.); life in a community of expatriate aid workers somewhat removed from the local population. These NGOs helped to frame the Calais migrant crisis as a public problem of international stature.

A dividing line appeared between them and the local mobilization networks, contrasting the volunteers on the ground with those humanitarian professionals on short-term missions. The former found it hard to accept the arrogance of the newcomers, who sometimes gave lessons on the right ways of doing things, even though their own knowledge of the local situation was only superficial. Their relations reproduced the tensions between volunteers and professionals that are well known in this field.[11] Yet they could not just be reduced to these: the humanitarian workers who intervened at Calais were young professionals, with a weak connection to the local organizations, but who nevertheless displayed the desire for dialogue and cooperation with these – by participating in meetings, or the establishment of common projects (such as the Médecins Sans Frontières centre for minors at Calais). Conversely, the professional organizations mandated by the state, who were specialists from the social sector rather than the international humanitarian one (such as La Vie Active or the AFEJI, and to a lesser extent France Terre d'Asile), remained somewhat apart from this local milieu, which was suspicious of their subordination to the public authorities.

New transnational solidarities: the 'accidental activists'

The new actors in refugee support who appeared at Calais from summer 2015 onwards, and to a lesser degree at Grande-Synthe and other encampments in the region, straddled the border between voluntary commitment and professionalization.

The new transnational solidarity expressed here was a real social phenomenon. Starting with the No Border camp of 2009, volunteers had come from different European countries to assist the migrants at Calais. In 2015, the phenomenon acquired an unprecedented scale: volunteers flooded into the Calais region from Belgium, Germany, Ireland, and above all the UK. In the UK, the cause of the Calais migrants attracted thousands of people, basically outside any formal structure, or in groups created ad hoc. This was the case with the founders of Help Refugees – three women, who had worked in arranging events, and who found themselves at the head of a wide organization of support for refugees after relaying the appeal for donations on behalf of the camp launched by a friend of theirs. Thanks to their networks, gifts poured in and they mobilized to organize distribution, but not until they themselves reached the camp in September 2015 did they decide to set up a real support system and remain on the site. They founded the association Help Refugees and linked up with the Auberge des Migrants, which lent them a warehouse. Their voluntary commitment became full-time, and they eventually started projects across Europe.

This transnational mobilization for Calais followed a heavy coverage of the 2015 'migrant crisis' in the European media, following the massive increase in Mediterranean crossings via Greece. Though nationalist and xenophobic reactions led to the borders of many European countries being closed, citizens also formed solidarity movements for a policy of welcome. The Franco–British border was the object of particularly intense media coverage in summer 2015, when intrusions into the Channel Tunnel proliferated, with migrants trying to cross the border along the rail lines and suffering serious and sometimes fatal accidents. The political declarations of tighter border control on the part of the British authorities were denounced by citizens' movements (for example, the Folkestone demonstration of August 2015); but it was above all the photograph of little Aylan, the Syrian boy drowned on the Turkish coast on 3 September 2015, which was widely shown in the British press, that triggered a wave of emotion and a broad movement of solidarity.

The mobilization mainly affected the south of England, geographically closer to Calais. But the London region, as well as other parts of the country (Birmingham, Glasgow, Manchester) also provided substantial numbers of volunteers.[12] These organized through social media (such as Facebook) and internet platforms such as Calaid-pedia[13] (which listed the collection points and convoys taking aid for the migrants), or other sites often referred to as 'people to people solidarity' to indicate their independence from pre-existing structures. The majority of volunteers arriving at Calais actually had no previous experience, either of voluntary work or of activism. This, however, did not mean that there were no networks spreading awareness and mobilizing. Besides the churches, citizens' networks such as Stand Up to Racism and Citizen UK played a major role in initiating mobilization and media coverage, all the more so as they had strong political connections in Jeremy Corbyn's Labour Party. Universities were privileged places of student mobilization, organizing not just collections, but also trips to Calais at weekends or in the vacations. Mobilization through networks in the world of entertainment also played an original role, with musicians and other performers finding the refugees a 'fashionable' cause, attractive to young people.

The new supporters had a younger profile, and often lacked any previous political or activist involvement. In an expression used by a newspaper article, they were 'accidental activists',[14] who had, so to speak, 'fallen' into the Calais cauldron. Their commitment sometimes went as far as a career change, with total dedication to the cause of the migrants. A growing politicization of their discourse was also noticeable, when their humanitarian action was opposed by decisions of the public authorities. This was particularly the case with the demolition operations conducted by the French authorities, which amounted to the destruction of everything the volunteers had built up with self-denial and generosity, and no recognition on the part of the state that they had made up for its deficiencies. This politicization also followed a more acute awareness of the contradictions of British policy on the international stage, and the human effects of the decision to reinforce border controls, a position still more strongly reaffirmed after the Brexit referendum of 23 June 2016. British volunteers organized both day-to-day humanitarian aid at Calais, and advocacy in London in support of accepting refugees.

For those who chose to stay at Calais for several months, the experience of assisting the migrants, and sometimes of total immersion in the encampment, amounted to a transformative experience, a moment of biographical rupture comparable to May 1968 or the experience of alternative lifestyles, which shaped consciousness and reoriented professional careers. Some people, disappointed by the attitude of the French authorities or believing they could be more useful elsewhere, decided to redeploy their activity to Greece. Calais might even be seen as an 'English Larzac',[15] with a strong effect on a whole generation.

Whatever the future holds, the transnational mobilization in support of the migrants at Calais will have been, by its scale alone, a major moment of cosmopolitan formation for many European supporters, who met local Calais activists with an involvement well anchored in regional and French political history, and encountered migrants and the 'world' of the Jungle, which both parties had contributed to shaping.

5

Destruction, dispersal, returns

If the Calais situation was the object of heavy media coverage, with a proliferation of reports and political interventions, including the condemnation of the state for the 'undignified' conditions of the Jungle, from winter 2015 the public authorities adopted a double strategy to empty the shantytown. This took the form of, on the one hand, police repression, with aggravated penalties for intruding on the ring road, and a multiplication of arrests and detentions in administrative centres, particularly ones remote from Calais (over a thousand people were dispersed across France at that point), and on the other, encouragement of asylum in France, making it easier to request asylum at Calais (a one-stop counter was opened in January 2016), and an offer of temporary accommodation for those who agreed to move into the ad hoc arrangements of the Centres d'Accueil et d'Orientation (CAOs) scattered across the whole country.[1]

'The biggest shantytown in Europe'

At Calais, a public order policy in the course of winter 2015 focused on the protection of the ring road to the port that ran adjacent to the shantytown, which was where migrants seeking to cross to England tried to board lorries. In January 2016, the decision was taken to destroy shelters on a '100-metre band' alongside the ring road, an operation described above from the standpoint of the organization of space in the Jungle (chapter 2, p. 40). But this no man's land was also intended to facilitate the work of the police in patrolling the road, now protected by fences topped with barbed wire, which were begun in April 2015 and by autumn 2016 had grown to a length of 3 kilometres, plus a further kilometre of concrete wall 4 metres high, completed in December 2016 after the destruction of the shantytown.

In February 2016, when the container camp for 1,500 people had just opened, the prefecture ordered the demolition of the southern zone of the shantytown. The land in this zone belonged to the Calais municipality, which forcefully demanded the expulsions, in the context of a rise in discontent and demonstrations in the town (the port management, the police unions, local far-right groups). National xenophobic movements were also active in Calais.

This partial demolition took place at the beginning of March. This far from put an end to the Jungle, which actually experienced a sharp rise in population in the course of spring 2016, reaching a peak of 10,000 by the end of the summer, rekindling political and media interest. The threshold effect was far from negligible, and the international press described the Jungle as 'the largest shantytown in Europe'. Though security measures at the Channel Tunnel and the ferry terminal had made the crossing to England more difficult, there were still frequent attempts to block traffic on the ring road, giving rise to several serious accidents.[2] Faced with pressure from the transport companies, the Calais town hall and an opposition that took advantage of the situation in the pre-electoral context, the government announced the definitive demolition of the camp by the end of the year.

These announcements, however, were made at different times, expressing disagreement between the various state bodies. At the local level, in fact, the position of the prefecture seemed to be that of seeking negotiated solutions with the voluntary organizations, in order to avoid the fiasco of February–March, when the violence of police intervention had made the front pages of the newspapers. Meetings were held from the spring onwards, in the course of which the organizations taking part in this dialogue with the authorities obtained the promise of appropriate solutions for all the migrants. In particular, agreement was reached that accommodation should not be dependent on making an asylum request; that there would be exoneration from the terms of the 'Dublin procedure' for those who wished to apply for asylum in France but had had their fingerprints taken in another country; and that particular attention would be paid to the situation of unaccompanied minors, with suitable accommodation arrangements being envisaged for these.[3]

On 29 August 2016, the transport companies, employers' organizations and trade unions announced a demonstration for 5 September, demanding the immediate demolition of the shantytown, which they blamed for their economic difficulties. Anticipating a strong turnout, the interior minister intervened to negotiate with the organizers of the demonstration and the municipality. At this meeting, on 2 September, he announced that the demolition would take place sooner than originally planned, but refrained from giving a date, despite the demands of the organizers. On 5 September the demonstration took place, but it was less strong than anticipated, and the CGT trade union federation refused to back its local dockers' branch, on account of their anti-migrant discourse.

In confirming the early date for expulsion, the right-wing newspaper *Le Figaro* published a plan by the interior minister to provide accommodation in several parts of France:[4] the demolition was presented as an operation of 'humanitarian sheltering'. It was supported by some of the main organizations active on the site, who were invited to inter-ministerial meetings, and requested at weekly operational meetings that an individual social assessment be conducted for each person affected. None the less, the supporters of the shantytown inhabitants were divided as to the position to adopt vis-à-vis the government's announcements. Some organizations approved of the project, as it would provide unconditional accommodation for all the residents on the site, and believed in the possibility of negotiating favourable conditions in terms of asylum requests. Others were suspicious of a police operation that aimed mainly at 'uprooting' the migrants. A demonstration in support of the migrants and against the destruction of the shantytown was organized for 1 October 2016 but banned by the authorities.

The pace accelerated when the Calais situation began to appear a political risk in the run-up to the presidential election. Reacting to the announcement of the dispersal of migrants from Calais to reception centres across France, hostile mobilizations were organized, for example by a coalition of mayors who came together under the slogan 'no migrants in my commune'.[5] Nicolas Sarkozy, a candidate in the right-wing primaries, visited Calais on 21 September 2016, denounced the inaction of the public authorities, and promised a demolition of the Jungle before summer 2017 if he was elected. On 25 September, President François Hollande outbid Sarkozy in announcing a demolition before the year end, and let it be understood that besides the shantytown, the two state reception centres would also be closed (the Centre Jules Ferry and the container camp).

These announcements took the local actors by surprise, all the more so as rumours circulated about the date of the operation, expected to begin in mid-October, which would not leave enough time for the social assessments demanded by the organizations, who were initially hesitant as to the right attitude to adopt. Finally, the majority of organizations who had originally supported the 'sheltering' project broke off dialogue and undertook legal action against the state. The hearings took place while the preparations for the expulsion were already under way, and the Lille tribunal rejected the request, holding that the operation envisaged did not violate the migrants' fundamental rights, but on the contrary aimed to ensure them more dignified conditions of accommodation, and that the organizations had no better alternative to propose. This defeat left the organizations divided and relatively powerless in the face of the impending evacuation, while any form of demonstration was prohibited.

Fearing resistance to the evacuation, the authorities decided to step up control of access to the site during the demolition operations. A 'protection zone' was established, based on the emergency legislation in force in France since the Paris attacks of 13 November 2015. This aimed to remove violent activists described as 'ultra-left', 'No Border' or 'Zadists'.[6] Representatives of the voluntary organizations had to request a badge before the operation began, and those that rejected this or had not been informed of the procedure in good time found themselves refused access. This measure further aggravated the confusion and divisions among the migrants' supporters, between those organizations that agreed to take part in the operation (by managing queues, accompanying migrants in the buses to the CAOs, or taking care of minors), despite in some cases declaring their disagreement with the operation, and those that opposed it completely.

Among the inhabitants themselves, the ambience in the run-up to the demolition was one of resignation. Though there was a palpable disquiet, the dominant feeling was one of powerlessness, and, in contrast to the mobilizations of the previous February against the demolition of the southern zone, opposition to the government's decision was only muted (see photo 10). The authorities took care to ensure the cooperation of the community leaders, who were charged with spreading appeals for calm and participation among their respective groups. These appeals were particularly broadcast in the Jungle's mosques, and their effect was that much better

Photo 10. Calais Jungle, 25 October 2016, the second day of the evacuation: awaiting departure for the Centres d'Accueil et d'Orientation (photo: Sara Prestianni).

as accelerated transfer to the United Kingdom for minors was promised in exchange.

The successive announcements of demolition, and the controls put in place in railway stations leading to Calais, led to a sharp fall in the shantytown's population in the weeks that preceded its destruction. The headcounts conducted by Help Refugees and the Auberge des Migrants showed 10,188 inhabitants in September 2016, but in October this was already down to 8,143. More than 2,000 people left Calais, and others did not bother coming at all, dissuaded by the prospect of the shantytown's destruction, fear of violence and arrest.

On the other hand, the number of unaccompanied minors increased in the same period, from 1,022 to 1,291, and in the end 1,900 young people were transferred to the 'Centres d'Accueil et d'Orientation pour Mineurs Isolés' (CAOMIs), to which should be added the 200 minors transferred to the United Kingdom before the start of the demolition. In March 2016, on the occasion of the Amiens summit, François Hollande and David Cameron had announced that unaccompanied minors with families in the United Kingdom would be speedily able to join these legally. In fact, it was a long time before procedures were set up; these took several months and led to about 700 transfers (including the 200 just before the demolition, with others sent to the CAOMIs). An amendment to the UK immigration laws in May 2016, known as the 'Dubs amendment',[7] envisaged the possibility of transferring to the UK unaccompanied minors from the refugee camps, on humanitarian grounds and even without proof that they had families there to take care of them. This arrangement, obtained thanks to pressure from British organizations such as CitizenUK, was not applied at all in summer 2016. When, in the week before the evacuation, the British authorities agreed to accept 200 young people, this accelerated operation aroused hope in many people, all the more so as the eligibility criteria were not precise. Thus, some sixty women were transferred to the UK on grounds of their vulnerability but without verification of their age, with the result that women from some encampments in the region hastened to Calais to benefit from a similar transfer. It was to avoid this kind of effect that the authorities decided to concentrate the demolition and 'humanitarian sheltering' operations in three days, starting on 24 October.

The sheltering operation as spectacle

A major element in this operation was the aspect of a spectacle, which was how it was conducted on the part of its organizers. A substantial communications mechanism was established by the prefecture authorities, who issued communiqués and invited journalists to press conferences. In the run-up to the demolition, these communications operations sought to show its humanitarian character. Thus, as well as the transfer of 200 unaccompanied minors to the UK, as already mentioned, the departure of eighty Calais migrants for Lille was shown to the press as a sign of the government's commitment to integration – these migrants had been accepted by the university and would be able to continue their studies there! Though the programme in question had been initiated by local voluntary organizations, the interior minister, visiting the Université de Lille on 20 October, presented it as his own initiative. In the course of the evacuation operation, a 'reception centre' was organized for the 700 or more accredited journalists and technicians, and guided visits around the operation's logistic arrangements were organized.[8] The demolition of the Jungle was an anticipated event that had aroused considerable attention on the part of the global media, and this found expression in the way that the evacuation of the site was turned into a spectacle. At the press conference held on the day before demolition, 23 October 2016, the prefect announced that in a few days 'the camp of La Lande will no longer exist, but there will be a dignified solution for each person concerned, and tomorrow they will be able to imagine their future anew'.

This exceptional operation of population displacement required a large-scale logistic mobilization, supported by the civil security division of the military and their disaster management operational centre. Fire brigades were also mobilized, as well as a total of 1,200 police and gendarmes. The prefecture requisitioned a hangar close to the shantytown, designated as an 'airlock' and designed to serve as a 'travel exchange', directing the evictees into buses for different destinations. Three waiting lines were planned: for adult men, for minors, and for the vulnerable (including women and families, sick and elderly persons). Inside the 'airlock', agents from the Office Français de l'Immigration et l'Intégration, supported by civil security personnel, would deal with everyone brought in and provide each with a coloured bracelet corresponding to their projected destination. This arrangement sought to show that each person's situation was taken into account. However, it was here that subsequent criticism would be focused, particularly as regards minors hoping for a possible transfer to the UK.

The operation was successful in communication terms, however, as in the first few days the smiling faces of candidates leaving for the CAOs were widely displayed in the media. Some fifty buses left Calais, or about one bus every 15 minutes, and the length of the queue that built up outside the hangar seemed to indicate the success of the operation.

Despite the heavy strength of the forces of order, their presence was relatively attenuated on the site of the 'protection' operation. Contrary to the previous days, and to the general police surveillance around the shantytown, they kept a relatively low profile, and it was the voluntary organizations, in particular Salam, Auberge des Migrants, Secours Catholique and Care4Calais, that regulated the queues and assisted individuals. Television was invited to film the start of the clearing operation, which officially began without clashes – despite the occupants having been evacuated by force, and witnesses alleging 'gas attacks' since the day before the clearing. In the following days, it was the fires that attracted considerable attention: impressive and photogenic, they provided the fascinating spectacle of a violent situation. These images might have belied the official narrative of a humanitarian operation conducted without coercion. But this narrative seemed to prevail, since at the end of the three days of the operation, the prefect announced its success, the 'sheltering' of all the migrants from the *camp de la Lande*', and interpreted the fires as departure customs in the 'culture' of the migrants.

The massive presence of the media served a government plan to show both the strength and the humanity of the public authorities. This presence also gave voice to unofficial parties that sought to draw media attention to their fate. This was the case, for example, with women, who demonstrated to demand admission to the UK, or the Oromos, an ethnic group persecuted in Ethiopia, who also organized a demonstration to publicize their cause. The migrants, preyed on by the media with its hundreds of lenses, could in some cases play on the situation to try and spread awareness of their condition or their demands. In the great spectacle of this humanitarian operation, however, these voices, like those of the voluntary organizations, were more or less drowned out.

The voluntary organizations, in fact, were quick to denounce serious dysfunction. From the first day, incidents broke out in the waiting lines, the organization of which was quite rudimentary. People were poorly informed, and the refusal of dialogue with the organizations familiar with individual situations did not permit an adequate orientation. The situation was particularly problematic for minors, or those claiming to be such, with several hundred crowding over one another in the hope of getting their situation examined by the Home Office agents.[9] In the week preceding the demolition, the British government had sent these out to deal with applications for transfer on the basis of the Dublin regulations (the presence in Britain of a family member who was a refugee or asylum seeker), or the Dubs amendment (criteria of vulnerability on grounds of age, nationality, risk of exploitation). This treatment was done very hastily, with young people being called by loudspeakers across the shanty-town to present themselves at the container camp. There was a great bustle, and tensions grew, with the UNHCR offering the help of its translators, the voluntary organizations helping to prepare the young people for the questions that they would be asked, and community representatives denouncing unfair treatment. Examination of the applications was suspended while the evacuation was under way. It was envisaged that all the minors would remain on the site, in the container camp, with their situation being examined in the days following the evacuation.

The rush of a large number of people into the line for minors created an overspill. It was then decided to separate beforehand those who 'looked like' minors from those who 'looked like' adults. Staff from the national office of France Terre d'Asile carried out this sorting at the entrance to the hangar, a practice that attracted much criticism. In principle, in fact, anyone who declared themselves a minor should have been entitled to an interview, and the choices made in emergency conditions did not permit individual situations to be assessed in a fair manner.

Those who were considered minors were placed in the container camp, in the centre of the Jungle, while waiting for the UK to rule on the possibility or not of their transfer. This emergency arrangement was contrary to the rules on protecting young people, and since it was supposedly temporary, professional support was seriously inadequate. Confusion about the prospects for transfer to the UK, and the lack of communication on the part of the Home Office agents, generated anxiety and violence, and incidents broke out, while some 200 young people who declared themselves minors did not have access to this arrangement, sleeping in what remained of the shantytown school, supported by volunteers from the organizations. These found it hard to attract media attention to the situation, whereas the prefecture announced that the humanitarian operation had been completed and all the inhabitants of the shantytown had been sheltered. Based on the count carried out before the operation by France Terre d'Asile, which showed 1,291 unaccompanied minors, the authorities calculated that after having accommodated more than 1,500 minors in the CAPs, and transferring over 200 to the UK, those who remained were no longer its responsibility. Their arrival was supposedly attracted by the opportunity of legal transfer to the UK.

For those adults who had refused to embark on the buses for the CAOs (either because they still hoped to cross to the UK, or fearing they would be sent to a department that was more severe in applying the Dublin regulations),[10] the authorities announced that they would be subject to 'control of their administrative situation', in other words, detention and removal, followed by forcible dispatch to their country of origin, or to a European country where their fingerprints had been taken. In fact, controls on the basis of appearance were frequent, often followed by arrest. Removal to detention centres was so frequent that the one in Coquelles was full, and buses were chartered to organize transfers to other centres, at Vincennes, Mesnil-Amelot, Strasbourg and Lyon.

The destruction of the shantytown was finished in the first week in November. The only people remaining on the site were the minors housed in the container camp (more than 1,500), and the women and children in the Centre Jules Ferry (more than 400). Though the British authorities had decided to suspend the examination of asylum applications at Calais, and the number of incidents among uncertain young people had risen, all the accommodation structures on the site were emptied. On 2 November, the young people still present, in the container camp and the church, were transferred to a CAOMI, accompanied by agents from the British Home Office. The following day was the turn for the evacuation of the women and children in the Centre Jules Ferry. With the closing of these reception centres, all the migrants on the site were dispersed across France.

Dispersal

The CAOs to which the Calais migrants were transferred were an exceptional arrangement, falling neither under regular emergency accommodation, nor accommodation intended for asylum seekers, a fact that expressed the proliferation of measures designed to meet the 'crisis'. The CAO system had been the object of experiment since October 2015, with the proclaimed aim of emptying the Calais Jungle by offering an accommodation option that was not dependent on making an asylum application, which it was supposed to favour by enabling migrants to make a pause on their trajectory. After a difficult start, as it imposed a major geographical removal, the arrangement subsequently met with a degree of success, inasmuch as it attracted Calais asylum seekers who had been victims of the saturation of dedicated accommodation.[11] In October 2016, it was decided to extend this system for the time being, in order to put a definitive end to the shanty-town: more than 7,500 places were thus made available at the end of October 2016, in more than 210 CAOs scattered across France (apart from the departments of Pas-de-Calais,

Corsica and Île de France), each with an average capacity of fifty. The interior and housing ministries worked together to open the places needed, as an emergency matter. State services were mobilized by way of the regional prefects, each called upon to find 800 to 1,000 places by a census of vacant sites: disused army barracks, retirement homes being refitted, holiday centres, etc. The staff of the asylum and social accommodation services were called upon to manage these sites, with a budget allocation of €25 per person per day. The CAO charter, drawn up in August 2016, laid down rules governing entrance and support, but the system was still very uneven, depending on the particular site, the presence or absence of a local framework of voluntary organizations, the availability of translators and lawyers, the distance from urban centres and the availability of transport facilities.

Problems of hostility from the local population in certain regions led to strong concern over possible acts of violence towards the migrants, who could be the object of xenophobic demonstrations.[12] They might well have improved their material conditions by leaving the shantytown, but they did not always have a sense of greater security; on the contrary, they no longer had the strength of numbers, or the reassuring presence of the strong support that they had in Calais. However, in the towns where they were settled, the arrival of migrants most often took place calmly, and the migrants suffered more from isolation than from attacks. Many municipalities organized to welcome the migrants, showing a dynamic of hospitality at the local level. Support networks were formed in various regions, thus continuing the solidarity expressed in helping migrants to settle, resolving logistic problems, or seeing that the authorities respected their commitments in terms of examining asylum applications.[13]

At the point that the Jungle was dismantled, the French authorities noted that a substantial proportion of the shantytown inhabitants were not actually seeking to reach the UK, but had requested asylum in France and were awaiting the allocation of housing; according to the Office Français de l'Immigration et de l'Intégration (OFII) [French Office of Immigration and Integration], close to half of those 'given shelter' when the Jungle was closed were in this situation.

A year later, 46 per cent had been given asylum in France. A major obstacle that the migrants came up against was the application of the Dublin regulations, which made the first EU country in which they arrived responsible for their asylum request. Under this provision, many people risked being sent back to Italy, Hungary or Greece.

The effect of the concentration at Calais, and the mobilization of voluntary organizations, had made it possible to negotiate with the authorities the non-application of the mechanisms of readmission, but no guarantee existed that commitments made verbally would be kept. Hence the serious worries of migrants in the CAOs, who often lacked information and saw that asylum seekers 'in the Dublin procedure' (those to whom the Dublin regulations were applied, forcing them to return to the first EU country in which they had arrived) were separated from those 'in normal procedure', whereas they had been promised that all could request asylum in France. Attempts were made at mobilization, particularly by resort to hunger strike. The migrants in the Rennes CAO, for example, published through their support collectives a communiqué in which they denounced the authorities' dispersal strategy: 'The government has tried to sell the Calais demolition as a humanitarian operation. All they did was disperse the migrants across the whole of France, so as to make their situation invisible and facilitate the management of procedures and expulsions.'[14] Dispersed across different sites, the migrants were less visible, and had a more restricted access to both the media and voluntary associations. Some CAOs, moreover, limited access to outside organizations and volunteers.

As far as minors were concerned, the CAOMIs were intended to be temporary. These centres did not come under the child protection regulations; they were a hastily set up ad hoc mechanism (the circular of the ministry of justice was published on 1 November, the day before the transfer of minors to the CAOMIs). They were supposed to house minors for the time it took for their situation to be examined by the British authorities; after three months, unaccompanied minors were to be transferred to the regular system of child protection. The lack of information and support for minors led to a number of them running away; in some CAOMIs, half the occupants left within a few days of their arrival. A month after the demolition, the question of the 'stabilization' of these young people arose once more, as on 9 December 2016 the Home Office indicated that it had finished examining the situation of unaccompanied minors and ended the transfer operations. A total of 750 young people had supposedly been transferred to the UK,[15] less than half of those present at the time of the demolition. When the end of transfers to the UK was announced, collective protest movements took place in the CAOMIs, including hunger strikes and demonstrations. In particular, there were numerous returns to Calais in the course of the winter, which gave an indication of the scale of the failure of this operation to help minors.

The 'sheltering' policy enabled the state to take back control of the situation, particularly by enabling it to deal with applications individually and avoid the mass effect that offered leverage to collective demands. By tackling the problem on a 'case by case' basis, the public authorities could thus restore their control over individuals.[16] The new accommodation sites would have the function not only of housing the asylum seekers but also of forced residence for those destined for expulsion.

After Calais, all the other informal encampments were targeted. A week after the Calais demolition, 3,800 people were evacuated from the Paris encampments, and likewise placed in emergency accommodation and CAOs. A transit centre was opened by the Paris city hall, to serve as an arrival 'airlock' while awaiting transfer to emergency accommodation. Given the lack of places, hundreds of people continued to camp, but were removed from Paris by the police. At Calais, migrants seeking to cross to the UK went into hiding, which meant they no longer had access to the services of humanitarian organizations.

The destruction of the Calais Jungle was undertaken in the name of public order and a humanitarian claim of providing accommodation worthy of human occupation. Though the 'sheltering' operation was quite exceptional in terms of its scale and speed, it did not amount to a genuine reception policy. This remained indeterminate, with the government alternating between openings and closures. The openings were an increase in the rate of recognition of refugee status,[17] and the limited but real establishment of a programme to resettle refugees coming from the Italian 'hot spots' or the camps in the Middle East.[18] The closures were a repressive security deployment at the border to prevent access to French territory and dissuade migrants in transit; identity controls on the basis of appearance and enforced placement in holding centres; the prosecution of volunteer helpers; and a more drastic application of the Dublin regulations, which enabled responsibility for the asylum application to be shifted to another state.[19]

After the demolition: returns and rejections

Already in the weeks leading up to the demolition, control by appearance, in principle illegal in France, was strengthened in the main railway stations from Paris to Calais. During the operation itself, a number of the police and gendarmerie mobilized for this had the task of preventing the arrival and re-establishment of migrants in the Calais region. When the demolition was completed, systematic controls by appearance were made in the three Calais stations, and were also frequent in the streets. These affected not only migrants but also non-white French residents, who were repeatedly subject to checks, often several times a day. Certain places such as parks were abandoned by people of colour. Gradually the law enforcers made a differentiation that was also based on appearance, between residents who looked foreign on the one hand, and individuals who looked like migrants on the other. From this point on, the direct checks became less systematic.

After the demolition, voluntary organizations reorganized their activities, focusing on patrols to seek out migrants, to distribute food at different places, especially on the edge of the town, and on a rather lesser scale, to document police abuses. Some of these activities continued to depend, as in the time of the shantytown, on volunteers who came to Calais from elsewhere in France, or from the UK. The solidarity of the local Calais population focused more on accommodation; there had never previously been so many offers of accommodation or migrants put up, mainly women, families and minors.

The visible pressure to prevent any re-establishment took its toll on the migrants, as well as on voluntary activity. The Calais town hall generally led the way in this, but the state soon followed, with the actions of the national police and with legal cover given to the prosecuting authorities for identity checks in certain districts. Here are two particular examples, concerning the migrants' access to showers and food supplies.

On 8 February 2017, Secours Catholique accepted delivery at its Calais offices of three shower units intended for the migrants. The chief secretary of the Calais mayor arrived with his personal vehicle, which he parked outside the entrance, preventing the unloading of the third shower unit. Shortly after, the municipality installed a skip for refuse in front of the entrance. Following a complaint by Secours Catholique, the administrative tribunal condemned the attack, and the town hall was forced to remove the skip and clear the access. The national police then took up the baton. They proceeded almost daily to arrest those migrants, particularly minors, who came to take showers. Three demonstrations at Calais, the arrest of a well-known woman journalist from a Secours Catholique vehicle that was transporting minors, and the arrival on the scene of a team sent by Jacques Toubon, the Défenseur des Droits,[20] brought an end to these checks and arrests.

On 2 March 2017, the Calais mayor issued a decree that banned unauthorized gatherings, explicitly targeting the distribution of meals in a zone on the edge of the town, where this took place on a daily basis. After the distribution point was moved outside this zone, the mayor issued a new decree on 6 March to extend the perimeter. When a number of voluntary organizations jointly took up the case, the administrative tribunal suspended the application of the two decrees. Once again, the national police took up the baton. Armed with an order from the prosecuting authorities, the police arbitrarily set a time for the distribution to end and then proceeded to identity checks and sometimes arrests, focusing either on the migrants or on the volunteers, which led to people dispersing. Over time, the situation grew worse, some food distributions being dispersed by the police without even the pretence of identity checks, sometimes with the use of tear gas. Sometimes the police would also intervene between the volunteers and the migrants, preventing the distribution from taking place. Volunteers carrying out patrols were likewise the object of frequent checks.

The new government that came in after the election of May–June 2017 continued this policy and even made it harsher. It made generous promises at the level of discourse. Thus, President Emmanuel Macron proclaimed on 27 July 2017: 'By the end of this year I no longer want men and women in the streets, in the woods. I want emergency accommodation everywhere.' On the ground, however, this promise was expressed in police harassment of the migrants present along the northern coasts. Though voluntary organizations noted the return of migrants to the Calais and Dunkirk regions from the start of 2017, the interior ministry proclaimed that its priority was to prevent migrants congregating at any fixed point around Calais or elsewhere on the coast. Despite court decisions that asserted the state's obligation to install water points and showers, and to authorize food distribution by voluntary organizations, on the ground it was the dispersal orders that prevailed, expressed on a day-to-day basis in the practices of harassing migrants, confiscating sleeping bags, using tear gas to coerce people or make meals unfit for consumption. The Auberge des Migrants/Help Refugees estimated that there were around 750 migrants still in Calais as of August 2017, chiefly young Afghan, Ethiopian and Eritrean men. At Grande-Synthe, after the fire at the humanitarian camp in April 2017, dozens of migrants were sleeping in the woods of Le Puythouck, in deplorable sanitary conditions. Over the summer their number rose from 200 to 400, with only a single water point installed in July. The police conducted dispersals, confiscations of tents and sleeping bags on a weekly basis, to prevent an encampment being re-established. While the mayor of Grande-Synthe, Damien Carême, was negotiating with the state to open a new reception site in his municipality, the interior minister Gérard Collomb decided to go ahead with a total evacuation of the site on 19 September: 564 individuals were 'sheltered' in centres scattered across France; four days later, some 400 of these had already returned. The encampment at Norrent-Fontes, located inland from Calais close to a motorway service station, was demolished the same week, on 18 September, despite a court decision of April 2017 having ruled against the expulsion of migrants, considering that the shelters they had there constituted their homes, as they gave protection from the weather and did not present a disturbance to public order.

Those who were expelled from the coastal area and then 'sheltered' in the CAOs, or the 'Centres d'Accueil et d'Examen de la Situation' newly established in the region, mostly returned to areas close to the crossing points, in the hope of reaching the UK, either because they had family and connections there, or because France, or other European countries they had gone through, did not allow them to request asylum, or did not view them as actual victims of persecution. This is why hundreds of Afghans whose asylum requests were dismissed in northern European countries, or Oromos arriving from Germany, returned to Calais. They took refuge at night in the woods, the *djangal*, forming little ephemeral 'jungles'.

Photo 11. Calais, 26 October 2016, the Jungle after evacuation and during its destruction (photo: Sara Prestianni).

Conclusion: the Calais event

What now remains of the Jungle that existed for a year and a half, from April 2015 to 26 October 2016, a few kilometres from the Calais town centre? Nothing, if we focus just on the landscape of desolation left by the bulldozers after its occupants had been removed and sheltered elsewhere, sometimes a long way from Calais (see photo 11). Absolutely nothing, if we are to believe the announcements by the mayor as to the future construction of an amusement park not far from 'la Lande', to attract tourists. Definitively nothing, to believe the effectiveness of the stubbornly repressive policy against migrants congregating at any fixed point in and around Calais, as practised by the government of Emmanuel Macron, the French president elected in May 2017. And yet, contrary to all this, a great deal remains if we look more deeply, as we have sought to do in the present study. We have attempted to understand what happened and what is still happening around this event, in Calais, in France and in the UK, and what it tells us about the position of migrants in Europe. The experience of the Calais Jungle offers several lessons for those who lived there, as well as for the town's inhabitants, for activists in voluntary organizations – local, British and European – for certain political movements and for everyone who made the Calais Jungle over many months the site of a real symbolic and political event.

The camp as hypertrophy of the border

This event, the Calais 'moment', was not just an unfortunate, detestable, shameful and unworthy episode in French policy, from many points of view, which one might hope to see forgotten as soon as possible, wiping out the country's recent history to reveal again the spirit of the Enlightenment, with its rather arrogant message to the rest of the world about the 'humanity' with which refugees should be treated. It is true, as many French political leaders declared, that the country need only challenge the Franco–British Le Touquet agreements of 2003 to put an end to this congestion on one side of the Franco–British border (in that case, the French side). But France did not do this. And to have the oxymoron of an excluding universalism accepted intellectually and politically, successive French governments had to repeat ad nauseam the phrase 'humanity and firmness', to distinguish good 'refugees' from bad 'migrants', as if these were natural categories, to value Syrian families rather than young Africans, to establish an a priori suspicion of any migrating individual, supposedly a threat and even a terrorist, and in this way stir up fear even before the Other, treated as an absolute stranger (alien), was able to give any sign of their history, their values or their situation, which might well have relativized this foreignness and brought them closer to sharing an equal humanity.[1]

But the hardening of the Franco–British border at Calais, and the policy of encampment, are not just part of a local and national history. Increasingly, throughout the world, the borders of nation states are tending to become tighter for certain categories of the foreign population, generally the most precarious and those coming from the countries of the South. Thus, even taken in their local and regional aspects, the Calais town and camp are part of a global movement. The number of people living today in some kind of camp or encampment can be estimated at 17 million worldwide. There are at least 6 million in official refugee camps (established under the aegis of the UN), or in camps for the internally displaced (established by national administrations or international NGOs), and both these figures have risen significantly in recent years with the dispersion of 5 million

Syrians and nearly 3 million Iraqis away from their countries
of origin, affected by the conflict under way in the Middle
East. There are also thousands of small encampments each
able to give temporary shelter to fifty or a hundred people,
sometimes more: at Idomeni on the border between Greece
and Macedonia in 2015–16, or around the port of Patras
in Greece between 1996 and 2009, several hundred people
in each case congregated around the border crossing points.
Similar camps are also found in cities – on waste land, in
ruins, in abandoned buildings, and all the urban interstices
– for example under the viaducts of the overhead Métro in
Paris. Likewise, in woods on the edge of border towns. The
camp created at Calais in April 2015 by the congregation
of migrants who had previously been scattered between a
number of encampments and squats in the town embodied
a particularly hybrid form of camp/shantytown. The investigation reported in this book has shown how central the
political question was, revolving around a permanent conflict
involving migrants, the state, and the voluntary organizations
of solidarity, to define the identity, meaning and function of
the site. The different ways of referring to it (camp, encampment, Jungle, New Jungle, *La Lande*, shantytown or even
state shantytown) reflect this conflict.

Calais has been a border town for centuries. Like many
border towns, it has seen camps, squats and 'jungles' of
migrants appear, disappear and reappear over the last fifteen
years, in the heart of the town, on its periphery, or more widely
in its region. From Lesbos through Ventimiglia to Calais,
migration routes are today strewn with camps, encampments
and refuges, their composition changing each day.[2] Study of
these shows an alternation between encampment and dispersal, which we also find in the history of the camps and
encampments of the Calais region since the late 1990s. A
kind of world thus develops in which the camps occupy a
special place, requiring collective investigation, both local
and global, critical reflection and the search for solutions
both within and beyond the camp form. A social reality as
much as a spatial one, the camp form is generally associated
with immobility, more precisely the immobilizing of people in
movement. In all these cases, an authority – local, national or
international – that exercises power over a territory decides

to put people in one form or another of camp, for a variable period, or forces them to form such a camp themselves. The site is distinguished from its environment by three criteria: extraterritoriality (a special space is physically delimited), exception (a legal and political regime that suspends regular citizenship) and exclusion (the encamped population is contained or repelled to the borders of the society).[3] The encampment, therefore, generally both signals and simultaneously conceals an excess population, above and left over from the sum of states. This is what the Le Touquet agreement produced, by envisaging the rejection by two neighbouring states of a migrant population that thus found themselves literally blocked between two borders, the camp in this case occupying the function of the border, or itself becoming a hypertrophy of the border.

Here again, the Calais case is simply one illustration – even if exacerbated, dramatic and seemingly exceptional – of a paradoxical movement within which a world is being built that is in fact increasingly global and supranational, triggering all kinds of mobility, but that in its representation and its government fails to emerge – does not yet know how to emerge – from the framework of national thought and action. In every case, with the foundation of camps and with their reproduction in the long term, there is a principle of excess, a surplus population. Not supernumerary in itself, in terms of the culture or identity of the migrants, but supernumerary in relation to what the governments of nation states are capable of thinking and doing vis-à-vis those men and women who find themselves placed outside of national frameworks, literally 'state-less' in the sense that the philosopher Hannah Arendt gave to this term, already associating it, more than sixty years ago, with the figure of the camp. As a German Jewish refugee who had herself been through the Gurs camp in southern France in 1940 before reaching the United States via Lisbon the following year, Hannah Arendt has inspired reflection on human rights: 'The Second World War and the D[isplaced] P[ersons] camps were not necessary to show that the only practical substitute for a non-existent homeland was an internment camp. Indeed, as early as the thirties this was the only "country" the world had to offer the state-less',[4] she wrote in 1951, the year that the UNHCR was founded. Pursuing critical reflection in this context, we can better understand the disastrous effects today of the epistemological nationalism of political thinking.[5] This lies at the root of a global-national political fiction, which is only able to realize itself at the price of violence towards the remainders it produces.[6]

It is only logical that this violence should find its place above all at the borders of nation states, where it targets a growing part of the world population, one that moves in precarious circulation, mainly from South to North, and finds itself blocked at the borders. This immobilization takes the form of spaces – camps, encampments, or illegal urban margins, always at the limit of legality, for example in the mode of 'tolerance' as was the case with the Calais Jungle – whose vocation is a priori to be invisible and to render their occupants equally invisible. Borders thus become an 'elsewhere' that is at the same time close at hand, and distant because difficult to access. Very close to these camps in this logic of exclusion are the dead (40,000 dead on the borders of Europe between 1993 and the start of 2017) and the subject of death itself.[7] By this, we mean the need to tell, count, identify and celebrate, often illegally, the dead who fell by the wayside in their attempt to cross borders.[8] As can be seen on the map of deaths on the Franco–British border (see map 3), for most of the time it is just a few metres, or a few hundred, from the Jungle, in the town and surroundings of Calais, that there are cases of falling (from the roof of a train or a lorry), crushing under lorries, or drowning, which cause the death of migrants who were living in the Jungle and trying to reach the UK despite the danger.

Cosmopolitics of the Jungle

In this context that is disturbing in so many ways, revolting as well as distressing, it has also been possible in this study to describe three major changes that took place in the framework of the Calais Jungle. First of all, a change in terms of the transformation and construction of private and public spaces, as described in chapter 2. As in the case of those shantytowns that it ended up resembling, the Jungle showed that even in

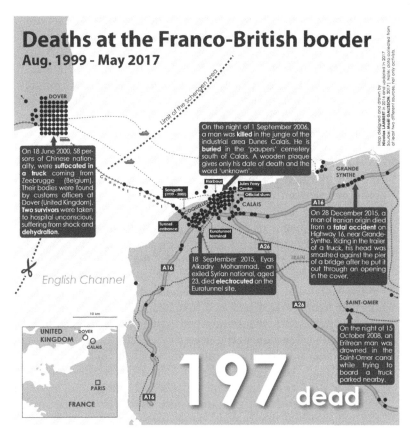

Deaths at the Franco-British border
Aug. 1999 - May 2017

On the night of 1 September 2006, a man was **killed** in the jungle of the industrial area Dunes Calais. He is **buried** in the 'paupers' cemetery south of Calais. A wooden plaque gives only his date of death and the word 'unknown'.

On 18 June 2000, 58 persons of Chinese nationality, were **suffocated in a truck** coming from Zeebrugge (Belgium). Their bodies were found by customs officers at Dover (United Kingdom). **Two survivors** were taken to hospital unconscious, suffering from shock and **dehydration**.

On 28 December 2015, a man of Iranian origin died from a **fatal accident** on Highway 16, near Grande-Synthe. Riding in the trailer of a truck, his head was smashed against the pier of a bridge after he put it out through an opening in the cover.

18 September 2015, Eyas Alkadry Mohammad, an exiled Syrian national, aged 23, died **electrocuted** on the Eurotunnel site.

On the night of 15 October 2008, an Eritrean man was drowned in the Saint-Omer canal while trying to board a truck parked nearby.

197 dead

English Channel

UNITED KINGDOM   DOVER
                  CALAIS

PARIS
FRANCE

Map 3. Deaths at the Franco-British border, August 1999–May 2017.

contexts of very great precariousness, it is not only possible but vital to *inhabit* sites, in other words to appropriate them, individually and collectively, and in this way produce a form of informal urbanization to which the great cities of the countries of the South are accustomed.

Secondly, a social, cultural and political life rapidly developed, bringing into mutual relationship migrants of some twenty nationalities and a dozen European ones. As we saw in chapter 3, a cosmopolitan microcosm formed here, around churches and mosques, schools, theatres and restaurants. In the same way, the 'Maison bleue sur la colline'

of the Mauritanian artist Alpha, who created the 'school
of arts and crafts' in the Jungle, or the white house of the
'International Journal' created by the political refugee from
Equatorial Guinea, Vicente,[9] became emblematic and attractive sites of a kind of 'experimental society'. The Calais Jungle
underwent the experience of a concentration of phenomena
of coexistence, conflict and collaboration, foreshadowing the
regular everyday life of the world to come.

Thirdly, in the domains of transformation and urbanization
of the space of the camp, as also of the social and political
life that developed within it, the relationship with solidarity
movements from Calais and Europe was essential, as shown
in chapter 4. Study of this relationship makes it possible to
observe and begin to understand – without judgement, and
far from the fearful fantasies widespread about migrants in
Europe – what the migrants bring to the life of the settled
citizens of Europe. The very numerous organizations and
individuals who mobilized on behalf of the Calais Jungle,
coming from Paris, London, Brussels and Europe in general,
established a form of commitment in which the cosmopolitan
aspect was a fundamental axiom.

Whether individual or collective, labelled 'humanitarian'
or 'political', this commitment to the sites where foreigners in a precarious situation had been shunted, and at the
same time, the cosmopolitan aspect of the site itself and
the relationships established there, question the new forms
of politics. On the one hand, they are a distant kin to the
various 'squares movements' that have marked political life in
many European and Arab capitals in the last few years. The
Calais camp was an occupation, or more precisely it became
so as time went on, although there was no 'convergence
of struggles' with the squares movements (and particularly
the movement of the Place de la République in Paris, 'Nuit
debout', which was partly contemporary with it). On the
other hand, this occupation has been the scene of a cosmo-
politics 'in situ'. Conversation, translation, learning and construction are words that precisely denote the exchanges that
took place on the Calais site. They are also terms that may
be associated with the idea of a 'common world' in the sense
of Hannah Arendt; in other words an intermediary space that
connects humans over and above all their singularities, thus

creating the free and public space of politics.[10] Finally, the politicization of migrants was a remarkable fact, generally minimized in commentaries that highlight the more familiar figures of victim and criminal, of fear and compassion. And yet, at Calais as at other sites of forced congregation, migrants blocked at the borders had a genuine political discourse. They politicized themselves against what to them appeared an injustice, a violence, and could be articulated as a conflict in the language of human rights, with such words as 'freedom', 'respect', 'humanity'. This is the common and universal language of politics. Unable to legally cross the border into the UK, unable to prevent the destruction of their shelters, schools, restaurants and shops when the first destruction of the southern zone of the camp took place in March 2016, standing up to police who were hostile on principle to their presence, the Calais migrants demonstrated on several occasions. They brandished posters and shouted slogans, in the streets and in the camp. Nine of them in fact went on hunger strike and sewed their lips together when the demolition of the southern zone of the camp was announced in March 2016. They distributed open letters denouncing the inhumanity of French and British policies, demanding the opening of borders and respect for human rights. Seeking an appropriate interlocutor, they even asked to meet representatives of the UN rather than representatives of the French administration.

The Calais Jungle thus acquired considerable significance.[11] A conflict of meanings was played out here, for all the actors and spectators of the Calais event, between disregard and consideration, compassionate emotion and empathic politics. Consideration gradually won the day, bit by bit, on this site that was initially illegitimate and undignified, then increasingly 'significant', successfully becoming a place of politics in a Europe already losing its bearings and seeking new mobilizing symbols. The political commitment that the Calais Jungle attracted in the form of solidarity from European citizens was particular in so far as it was based on empathy, an approach that seeks to understand as closely as possible the meaning of the Other's existence, the Other who arrives and even presses at the border, forcing the settled population to consider this new subject, blocked in the border-camp.

And in this exchange, the settled discover that the 'outsiders' (those coming from outside) have their own politics, based on their own experiences, experiences of the countries from which they come and of the world of migration in which they have found themselves for months or years. This is certainly the cause, or one of the causes – the most political one – behind the destruction of the Jungle and the dispersal of its inhabitants.

A final aspect, just as important in the formation of a common world in the space of the Calais Jungle as border, is the fact that a relationship of 'mutual respect' was gradually established, at the request of the migrants, between them and those coming in their support (described in chapter 4). In order to avoid behaviour that was too intrusive or even disrespectful, representatives of the major communities in the shantytown (Afghan, Sudanese, Kurds, Eritreans, Ethiopians, Syrians, Egyptians, Iraqis) described and handed to the NGOs and voluntary organizations a 'good conduct code' applicable in the Jungle. This meant that the Jungle had indeed become (or was in the process of becoming) their refuge, their hearth and home, thereby shifting the usual terms of hospitality, with the relationship between host and guest being in a way rebalanced and becoming rather more egalitarian. The strangers who were there and had made this site more familiar for themselves wanted to receive as their 'guests' the inhabitants of those very territories from which they were excluded. This way of acting, of inhabiting the site and rendering it welcoming according to a code of conduct acceptable to both sides (welcomers and welcomed) could then become both a factor of openness of the site at the same time as a lesson in hospitality.

The eighteen months of existence of the Jungle saw a complex apprenticeship in coexistence and collaboration, in 'living together' and 'working together'. Initially, the transfer of migrants to this site, transformed into a resettlement camp, seriously inhibited the relationship between migrants and those Calais residents involved in solidarity organizations. But what then happened both illustrates and confirms a way of acting that is increasingly widespread in the worlds of mobility, one adapted to precarious situations, police constraint and uncomfortable dwellings, and that by this process of adaptation transforms them so as to make even this life sometimes a habitable one. They were feeling better on this site, which ended up deserving its name of 'shantytown' rather than simply 'camp'. It could become a town and a community. With this shantytown/camp, the migrants themselves invented the hospitable town in France that the government refused them.

It was against this that the state finally reacted, against this camp that little by little emerged from the shadow and became too visible, autonomous and political.

Postscript: how this book was written

The project for this book was born in June 2015 during a lively conversation between John Thompson and Michel Agier at a café terrace on the rue de Rennes in Paris, near the École des Hautes Études en Sciences Sociales, at which it became very clear that Calais was a complex Franco–British problematic that deserved a comprehensive social science intervention. But everything was still to be done. The research and collaborative project began in early 2016, when the selection by the Agence Nationale de la Recherche (ANR 2016–2019) of the project *Babels – La ville comme frontière* (http://anrbabels.hypotheses.org/) made it possible for this to be undertaken, at a time when the Calais 'Jungle' was nearly halfway through its existence. But it was already obvious, by research and participation that various people had conducted on site, that something exceptional was happening, on a European scale, and that the perspective of social science was needed, on top of that of journalists, artists or political leaders, in order to offer a description and in-depth analysis of the event and its significance. Relationships that had long been established between researchers, students and actors in the Calais voluntary organizations made it possible to develop a plan for the work collectively, by way of successive meetings and while the investigation was under way. Chapters or sections of chapters were entrusted to one or more people, and the completed text was circulated among all the participants.

The authors

Michel Agier, anthropologist, director of studies at the École des Hautes Études en Sciences Sociales and senior researcher at the Institut de Recherche pour le Développement, has carried out research on refugees, migrants and borders. His fieldwork studies took him away from France (*desplazados* in Colombia, refugees and displaced persons in Kenya, Zambia and West Africa, migrants and refugees in Lebanon), before he pursued the same focus in Europe and finally at Calais. He is a member of the Migregroup platform for researchers and voluntary organizations. He coordinated the project of this work by mobilizing and bringing together individuals from both an academic background and from voluntary organizations. These two perspectives constantly intersected on the ground. The distinction is not always obvious, as the four participants in this work who are seen rather as 'activists' or campaigners have been very reflective, concerned for the accuracy of the information they receive and regularly write up (blogs, newspaper articles or chapters in a book). On the other hand, the majority of researchers who contributed to this book regularly work with voluntary organizations. Michel Agier, in particular, wrote the introduction and conclusion, and coordinated and harmonized the writing of the whole book.

Yasmine Bouagga, a sociologist conducting research at the CNRS (Laboratoire Triangle-ENS Lyon), carried out a field study in the Calais Jungle from February to October 2016, continuing this after the demolition. Her project was originally designed to support the cartoonist Lisa Mandel in the context of the Appel de Calais. As a way of depicting the situation, they created a cartoon blog, *Les Nouvelles de la Jungle*, published on LeMonde.fr, leading on to a picture book published by Éditions Casterman in 2017. Over several months, this reportage became an ethnographic study of the migrants, their supporters and the public authorities: the object was to understand how this unlikely and unstable society of the Jungle was organized. Yasmine Bouagga joined the collective research programme Babels, for which she coordinated the collective work *De Lesbos à Calais, comment l'Europe fabrique des camps* (Éditions du Passager Clandestin, 2017). In the present work, she wrote chapter 3 on everyday life in the shantytown, part of chapter 4 on solidarities (with Mathilde Pette), and chapter 5 on the dispersal (with Philippe Wanneson).

Maël Galisson was for three years (June 2012–May 2015) coordinator of the Plateforme de Service aux Migrants, a network of organizations in support of refugees in the north of France (http://www.psmigrants.org/site/). In this context, he coordinated with Mathilde Pette the dossier 'Violence d'État contre les exilés de Calais', published in *Libération* in July 2014. He also participated in the creation and regular publication of the *Journal des Jungles*, a periodical jointly conceived by refugees and volunteers (eight issues appeared between September 2013 and March 2017). In the wake of this experience, he spent several months conducting a study of migrants who died on (and because of) the Franco–British border. In the present work, Maël Galisson chiefly contributed to writing chapter 1, in which the episode of 'the' Calais Jungle is placed in a wider historical and geographical context. He was also involved in conceiving the three maps drawn by the geographer Nicolas Lambert.

Cyrille Hanappe is an architect and engineer, lecturer and educational director of the Diplôme de Spécialisation en Architecture des Risques Majeurs at the École Nationale Supérieure d'Architecture Paris Belleville. He is a member of the architectural agency AIR, and also chair of the professional association Actes & Cités, which works for the dignity of people in their context of life. After working for several years on shantytowns in Latin America, then in Île-de-France, he began to involve himself in the squats and encampments of the Calais region in 2014, and helped to set up the Maison du Migrant, a concept initiated by voluntary organizations coming together around the Plateforme de Service aux Migrants. Cyrille Hanappe wrote chapter 2, on the architecture and habitation of the jungles, squats and camps.

Mathilde Pette is a sociologist, and since 2016–17 lecturer at the Université de Perpignan Via Domitia. She was born in and studied at Lille, where she presented a thesis in 2012 on the voluntary organizations and activists supporting foreigners in this region. She went on to pursue her research in the context of a post-doctoral study on organizations assisting migrants wishing to reach the UK who found themselves blocked at the Franco–British border. In parallel with her academic activity, she has worked with local organizations to initiate collective projects such as popular education workshops and inter-organizational forums. She was recently joint curator of the photographic exhibition 'Ceux qui passent, ceux qui restent. Le campement de migrants de Norrent-Fontes', together with the photographer Julien Saison/O2e and volunteers from Terre d'Errance. In this book, she wrote chapter 4 on forms of solidarity (with the assistance of Yasmine Bouagga and Madeleine Trépanier).

Philippe Wannesson's previous professional career was in the field of social work and popular education. He came to Calais in December 2008 for a workshop on the refugee situation and settled there in April 2009 to engage in solidarity actions. He is involved in the local voluntary network (the organizations La Marmite aux Idées and Le Réveil Voyageur), and a member of the Migreurop network. He founded and edits the blogs Passeurs d'hospitalités (https://passeursdhospitalites.wordpress.com/ and https://passeursdhospitalitesenglish.wordpress.com/), an essential means of information and alert that aims to provide refugees with tools to assist their independence and organization, to inform and sensitize people about the situation of migrants at Calais and in the region, and to challenge the public authorities and participate in the network of various activists. On the basis of his intimate knowledge of the local history of migrations, he wrote chapter 1, which gives a chronology of migration policy and violence in the region (with Maël Galisson) and helped with chapter 5 on the dispersal.

Five other people also made important contributions to this work. Madeleine Trépanier, an anthropology student at the EHESS, carries out research at Calais on the solidarity of British organizations, and contributed on this basis to chapter 4. Céline Barré has worked since 2014 in voluntary organizations, Calais-based and international, that help with the reception of migrants and asylum seekers (Secours Catholique, Médecins du Monde, Bibliothèques Sans Frontières). For the present book, she shared with the whole team her experience and knowledge of present-day migration routes, the creation of the last Jungle and the role of voluntary organizations. Sara Prestianni, formerly coordinator of the Migeurop platform and currently of the Italian organization ARCI, shared with the team her knowledge of the 'jungles' of Calais and Europe over the last twelve years. She is also a photographer (https:// www.flickr.com/photos/saraprestianni/), has curated several photo exhibitions on the worlds of migration and camps, and she contributed her photos of the Calais Jungle to the present book. Similarly, Julien Saison, a photographer working with the refugees, has been kind enough to provide his photos of the Norrent-Fontes encampment. Finally, the geographer Nicolas Lambert, a research engineer at CNRS specializing in European cartography, created the three maps in this book showing the Schengen boundaries, migrant settlements in the Calais region, and deaths on the Franco–British border.

Notes

Introduction: for a better understanding

1 In the context of the research programme 'Babels – La ville comme frontière', supported by the Agence nationale de la recherche (ANR). For a presentation of the team that authored this book, see the Postscript.

2 See Babels, *De Lesbos à Calais. Comment l'Europe fabrique des camps* (ed. Yasmine Bouagga), Lyon: Éditions du Passager Clandestin, 2017.

3 See Babels, *La Mort aux frontières de l'Europe: retrouver, identifier, commémorer* (ed. Carolina Kobelinsky and Stéfan Le Courant), Lyon: Éditions du Passager Clandestin, 2017.

4 As the authors themselves later note, smuggler (*passeur* in French) is hard to define, and this is still harder in English. It 'can cover both the bosses of mafia groups and those individuals who occasionally share a good scheme in exchange for remuneration, or again those who pay for the cost of their crossing by helping to close lorry doors or block the motorway.' Some voluntary organizations helping refugees now also describe themselves as *passeurs* [Translator's note].

5 See the study by Sophie Djigo, *Les Migrants de Calais. Enquête sur la vie en transit*, Marseille: Agone, 2016; the Europe-wide reportage of Fabienne Brugère and Guillaume Le Blanc, *La Fin de l'hospitalité. Lampedusa, Lesbos, Calais… jusqu'où irons-nous?*, Paris: Flammarion, 2017; and the reflections on the

Calais Jungle in an essay on significant extraordinary spaces across the world by Michel Lussault, *Hyper-lieux. Les nouvelles géographies de la mondialisation*, Paris: Seuil, 2017. Also the blog *La 'Jungle' et la 'ville'*, published by Camille Louis and Étienne Tassin since February 2016 (https://blogs.mediapart.fr/Jungle-et-ville/editions/articles), and the issue devoted to the Calais Jungle, 'Migrants/Habitants: urbanités en construction', *Multitudes*, 64, autumn 2016.

6 In October 2015, 800 filmmakers, writers, artists and intellectuals called on their colleagues to visit Calais and lend their support and contribution to the Jungle's existence (http://www.liberation.fr/france/2015/10/20/Jungle-de-calais-l-appel-des-800_1407520).

7 See *Décamper. De Lampedusa à Calais, un livre de textes et d'images & un disque pour parler d'une terre sans accueil* (ed. Samuel Lequête and Delphine Le Vergos, preface by Michel Agier, Paris: La Découverte, 2016). Also Henk Wildschut's photographic essay, *Ville de Calais*, Guingamps: Éditions GwinZegal, 2017, and the novel by Delphine Coulin, *Une fille dans la Jungle*, Paris: Grasset, 2017. Again in the context of the Appel des 800, the cartoonist Lisa Mandel and the sociologist Yasmine Bouagga produced a comic book *Nouvelles de la Jungle* (Paris: Casterman, 2017). Films made in the context of this solidarity movement include the documentary *Nulle part en France* (Arte, March 2016) by the actress and stage director Yolande Moreau, with a text by the writer Laurent Gaudé. See also the project 'Réinventer Calais' on the website of the Perou association, which presents the work of several photographers, documentary filmmakers, architects and writers about the Calais Jungle (https://reinventercalais.org/). In the UK, the book *Voices from the 'Jungle': Stories from the Calais Refugee Camp* (ed. Marie Godin, Katrine Møller Hansen, Aura Lounasmaa, Corinne Squire and Tahir Zaman, London: Pluto Press, 2017) brought together texts by migrants who had lived in the Calais Jungle for a few weeks or several months. These texts were prepared in the context of courses given by a team of teachers from the University of East London in the Calais Jungle on the theme 'life stories in the Jungle'. This project gave rise to a kind of writing workshop. Some of the texts were written directly by the migrants, others transcribed by the editors on the basis of interviews, sometimes revised by the authors. The extracts of the transcriptions and texts are introduced and commented on by the editors; they speak of the itineraries of the refugees, their feelings about life in the camp, and their hopes for the future.

8 See, in particular, Terry M.S. Evens and Don Handelman (eds.), *The Manchester School: Practice and Ethnographic Praxis in Anthropology*, New York and Oxford: Berghahn Books, 2006.

Chapter 1. Movement to and fro: the Calais region from 1986 to 2016

1 This would later become the Collectif de Soutien d'Urgence aux Refoulés et aux Réfugiés, formed in 2016 by a number of organizations: AC!, Action Catholique Ouvrière, Artisans du Monde, La Belle Étoile, Emmaüs, Ligue des Droits de l'Homme, Mission Étudiante, Pastorale des Migrants and Les Verts.

2 http://www.interieur.gouv.fr/rubriques/c/c2_le_ministere/c21_actualite/02_09_27_sangatte

3 Speech by interior minister Nicolas Sarkozy, on the occasion of the Assises des libertés locales de la région Poitou-Charentes at Futuroscope, near Poitiers (Reuters, 9 November 2002).

4 Direction Départementale de la Police Aux Frontières (DDPAF), 2003 report.

5 Violaine Carrère, 'Au square. Le Collectif de soutien aux exilés du 10ᵉ arrondissement de Paris', *Vacarme*, 25, 2003, 112–16.

6 See Michel Agier and Sara Prestianni, *Je me suis réfugié là! Bords de route en exil*, Paris: Éditions Donner Lieu, 2011.

7 This encampment was destroyed in September 2017. Several dozen people rebuilt an encampment in a nearby wood.

8 Statutes of the Réseau des Élus Hospitaliers.

9 Letter from the Pas-de-Calais prefecture, *Mise en place d'une table-ronde sur la situation des populations de migrants dans le Pas-de-Calais*, 28 December 2012.

10 Circular of 26 August 2012 regarding preparation and support for operations of evacuating illegal encampments.

11 'Maisons des migrants: un appel à candidatures pourrait être lancé aux communes du Calaisis', *La Voix du Nord*, 18 December 2013: http://www.lavoixdunord.fr/region/maisons-des-migrants-un-appel-a-candidatures-pourrait-ia33b48581n1785201.

12 'Agressions contre des migrants à Calais: du ferme pour les quatre skinheads', *Le Phare dunkerquois*, 13 November 2010: http://www.lepharedunkerquois.fr/actualite/Faits_Divers/2010/11/13/groupe-nord-littoral-1307649.shtml

13 'Calais: Natacha Bouchart "comprend" le maire de Croix et établit un parallèle entre Roms et migrants', *La Voix du Nord*, 17 September 2013.

14 'Sauvons Calais' Facebook page.

15 Ibid.

16 The generic name for French volunteers in the Wehrmacht and Waffen-SS during the Second World War [Translator's note].

17 'Calais: les néonazis dans le viseur', *Libération*, 19 September 2014: http://www.liberation.fr/societe/2014/09/19/calais-impunite-pour-les-neonazis_1104308

18 http://www.unitesgppolice.com/sites/default/files/pdf/2014-10
   -01_Rassemblement_Calais.pdf
19 'Sept personnes, dont cinq du Calaisis, interpellées à Loon-Plage:
   "ils étaient en chasse pour agresser des migrants"', *La Voix du Nord*,
   11 February 2016: http://www.lavoixdunord.fr/region/sept-
   personnes-dont-cinq-du-calaisis-interpellees-a-ia33b0n3325030
20 See Philippe Wannesson, '*Calais, les murs et la ville*', *Raison
   présente*, 202 ('Un monde emmuré'), 2nd quarter 2017, 67–75.

Chapter 2. From Sangatte to Calais: inhabiting the 'Jungles'

1 Olivier Clochard, *Le Jeu des frontières dans l'accès au statut de
  réfugié. Une géographie des politiques européennes d'asile et
  d'immigration*, Université de Poitiers, 2007. See also the docu-
  mentaries 'Sangatte, Station Balnéaire' (a film by Nadia Boufer-
  kas, Wasila Zahzouma, Benjamin Durand, Nicolas Potin, 2002,
  available at https://vimeo.com/37976568) and 'Welcome Out/In
  Sangatte' (by Florence Pezon, 2002).
2 Ibid.
3 See Coordination Française pour le Droit d'Asile, *La Loi des
  Jungles*, Paris, 2008, p. 42.
4 We shall return in chapter 3 to the strategies deployed in border
  crossing attempts.
5 A gloss on the slogan 'la France terre d'asile' [land of asylum],
  the 'M' at the end here standing for *merde*, i.e. shit.
6 This was a book by the Austrian architect Camillo Sitte,
  originally published in 1889 (*The Art of Building Cities: City
  Building According to Its Artistic Fundamentals*, Martino Fine
  Books, 2013). A 'classic' familiar to all architects, it proposed
  a rediscovery of the architecture of medieval European towns,
  as against the classical and 'orthonomic' town of Louis XIV's
  France. It stressed the spatial and aesthetic qualities of their
  unplanned urban forms.
7 Elise Vincent, 'Calais va rouvrir un centre d'accueil pour
  migrants', *Le Monde*, 3 September 2014.
8 'Migrants à Calais: un nouveau terrain d'accueil à côté du
  Centre Jules-Ferry', *La Voix du Nord*, 7 March 2015.
9 'Migrants de Calais: un camp "toléré" voit le jour autour du
  centre Ferry', *La Voix du Nord*, 24 March 2016.
10 The term used by the Service Public at the Centre Jules Ferry
   and the Centre d'Accueil Provisoire.
11 Sitte, note 6 above. See Cyrille Hanappe, 'La Jungle de Calais –
   laboratoire de la ville de demain?', *Urbanisme*, 406, autumn 2017.

Chapter 3. A sociology of the Jungle: everyday life in a precarious space

1 A study conducted from February to October 2016 by Yasmine Bouagga, with the support of the Babels programme and the Laboratoire Triangle-CNRS.
2 On 31 August 2016, La Vie Active housed 209 women and 90 children on the site.
3 See the report *Ni sains ni saufs*, published in June 2016 by the association Trajectoires on behalf of UNICEF: https://www.unicef.fr/sites/default/files/atoms/files/ni-sains-ni-saufs_mna_france_2016.pdf
4 On the importance of these kitchens in the everyday life of the camp, see chapter 4, p. 98.
5 For example, a violent brawl in May 2016 led to some forty people being wounded, and 200 shelters set on fire.
6 The Jungle Books Kids Restaurant was itself an example of reconversion from an economic activity to a humanitarian one, when the owner of the Kabul Café, following a fire that destroyed his restaurant, joined with the founder of the library-school Jungle Books to serve up to 200 free meals each day to unaccompanied minors.
7 The question of prostitution is not confined to trafficking networks, and the boundaries are often fuzzy between the search for a protector and income, and the exploitation of a vulnerable situation.
8 Data from 29 September 2016 (source: Police aux Frontières). This body's zone of competence extends to the ports of Calais and Dunkirk, as well as to the Channel Tunnel.
9 See, for example, 'Migrants à Calais: les chiffres de la délinquance explosent, selon un syndicat de police', *La Voix du Nord*, 13 October 2014.

Chapter 4. A Jungle of solidarities

1 The term 'association' is a status provided for by a French law of 1 July 1901, referring to a group of people coming together with a non-profit objective.
2 By 'volunteer', we mean those individuals engaged in a collective or association without receiving either direct or indirect remuneration for their services. The term 'activist' refers to both volunteers and paid staff working for associations.
3 Standing for 'Soutenons, aidons, luttons, agissons pour les migrants et les pays en difficulté'.

4 The Collectif de Secours aux Réfugiés (C'SUR, pronounced as 'c'est sûr') was founded in 1997 to combine various solidarity associations (such as Secours Catholique and Emmaüs) as well as legal defence associations. See chapter 1.

5 Salam decided on a 'hunger strike' to force the state to intervene in support of the migrants.

6 We can mention among others the SOAS 'Music Room' project, and that of the École Nationale Supérieure d'Architecture de Paris-Belleville (some of whose work is included in chapter 2 of the present book), also master's courses in geography at Université de Tours and the EHESS Master in Comparative Studies on Development.

7 Gaedig Bonabesse, the organization's president, explained: 'I went to Calais with my partner, and we were swept up in a hurricane of emergency. Returning home in December we set up the association with a group of people working in voluntary organizations and event management, since unfortunately support from the state is so inadequate that every contribution is useful' ('Utopia 56. Intervenir auprès des migrants à Calais', Le Télégramme, 13 January 2016).

8 With the same legal status as other associations, professional associations are commissioned by the state to carry out missions of public service.

9 https://passeursdhospitalites.wordpress.com/

10 http://calais-ouverture-humanite.e-monsite.com.

11 Mathilde Pette, S'engager pour les étrangers. Les associations et les militants de la cause des étrangers dans le Nord de la France, doctoral thesis in sociology, Université de Lille, 2012, and Pette, 'Calais: les associations dans l'impasse humanitaire?', Plein Droit, 2015/1, 104, 22–26.

12 See Madeleine Trepanier, 'Les Britanniques à Calais. La solidarité européenne à l'échelle locale dans une ville frontière', Multitudes, 64, autumn 2016, 82–91.

13 A contraction of 'Calais' and 'aid'.

14 'Accidental Activists: the British women on the front line of the refugee crisis', Guardian, 12 June 2016.

15 The reference is to a non-violent civil disobedience action by farmers resisting the extension of an existing military base on the Larzac plateau in South Western France. The action lasted from 1971 to 1981, and ended in victory for the resistance movement when the newly elected President François Mitterrand formally abandoned the project [Translator's note].

Chapter 5. Destruction, dispersal, returns

1 With the exception of Pas-de-Calais, Corsica and Île-de-France.

2 For the location of the 197 deaths on the Franco–British border from August 1999 to May 2017, see map 3 on p. 139. Since 2015, some forty migrants have died at this border – on the motorway, the ring road, or in the Channel Tunnel. See also Babels, *La Mort aux frontières de l'Europe: retrouver, identifier, commémorer* (ed. Carolina Kobelinsky and Stefan Le Courant), Lyon: Éditions du Passager Clandestin, 2017.

3 Christened 'Amina', this project of a reception centre for minors with 72 places was confirmed in late summer.

4 The figure of 12,000 places was put forward in *Le Figaro*, but in the end about 7,500 places would be made available.

5 This was the name of an association set up by the Front National mayor of Hénin-Beaumont, Steeve Briois, on 16 September 2016. Two days previously, the president of the Rhône-Auvergne region, Laurent Wauquiez, a member of the main right-wing party Les Républicains, had offered to 'support the mayors in their acts of resistance' to the government's plan to distribute the Calais migrants in centres across the whole of France.

6 The terms of the decree mentioned the 'far-left "No Border" activists', while the fear of 'Zadist' activists, spread by the local press (*Nord Littoral*, 20 October 2016), referred to activists conducting occupations of a zone and defending it against police operations, such as at Notre-Dame-des-Landes in the west of France, where since 2009 this mobilization had blocked an airport construction project.

7 Section 67 of the Immigration Act 2016. This amendment was named after Lord Dubs, who had himself arrived in Britain as a child on the Kindertransport to rescue Jewish children just before the Second World War.

8 Some journalists, however, were refused accreditation, and four (including three British) were even arrested and detained.

9 After incidents when the police used truncheons to try and control the line of young people, the forces of order in practice delegated this management to the voluntary organizations.

10 Many asylum-seekers had had their fingerprints taken in another EU country, making the latter responsible for examining their application, according to the Dublin regulations, though departmental prefects could still suspend expulsion at their discretion.

11 In particular, the saturation of the Centres d'Accueil pour Demandeurs d'Asile, which had a capacity of 38,000 places in 2016 for the whole of France, and of the complementary emergency shelters, making a total of about 50,000 places, according to the Office Français de l'Immigration et de l'Intégration (OFII) responsible for their management.

12 For example, a hostile poster campaign on the part of the Béziers town hall, divisions within the town of Alleix, and direct attacks against reception centres.

13 La platform 'Le sursaut citoyen' counted in April 2017 nearly a thousand local initiatives of solidarity with the migrants (https://sursaut-citoyen.org/).

14 Communiqué of 16 November 2016. Migrants accommodated in the Rennes CAO, who were notified of an order to expel them to Italy, in the context of a 'Dublin readmission', decided to embark on a hunger strike.

15 Amelia Gentleman and Lisa O'Carroll, 'Home Office stops transfer of Calais child refugees to UK', *The Guardian*, 9 December 2016: https://www.theguardian.com/uk-news/2016/dec/09/home-office-transfers-of-calais-child-refugees-to-uk-cease

16 We can compare this with the ways in which mobilizations of other undocumented migrants were resolved, prioritizing paths of regularization on a case-by-case basis and applying specific criteria, rather than blanket solutions.

17 A total of 85,244 asylum applications were made to the OFPRA in 2016, against 80,075 in 2015; 36,233 individuals received protection in 2016, against 26,818 in 2015 (https://www.ofpra.gouv.fr/fr/l-ofpra/actualites/premiers-chiffres-de-l-asile-en-0).

18 In the context of the European relocalization plan, France committed itself to accept 30,000 migrants between September 2015 and September 2017; by April 2017, it had accepted 16,554, slightly more than half. On top of this number of relocalizations from Greece and Italy were around 2,000 refugees resettled from the camps in Lebanon, Jordan and Turkey.

19 France undertook 25,963 'Dublin referrals' in 2016, against 11,657 in 2015 and 4,948 in 2014.

20 The government ombudsman [Translator's note].

Conclusion: the Calais event

1 On the conditions of granting the title of refugee and the absence of a 'correct' definition of administrative categories past and

present, see Michel Agier and A.-V. Madeira (ed.), *Définir les réfugiés*, Paris: PUF, 2017.

2 See Babels, *De Lesbos à Calais. Comment l'Europe fabrique des camps* (ed. Yasmine Bouagga), Lyon: Éditions du Passager Clandestin, 2017.

3 Michel Agier, *Managing the Undesirables: Refugee Camps and Humanitarian Government*, Cambridge: Polity, 2011, and *Un monde de camps* (edited together with Clara Lecadet), Paris: La Découverte, 2014. On the camp form, see Marc Bernardot, 'Les mutations de la figure du camp', in O. Le Cour Grand-maison, G. Lhuilier and J. Valluy (eds.), *Le Retour des camps? Sangatte, Lampedusa, Guantanamo*, Paris: Éditions Autrement, 2006, pp. 42–55); Maria Muhle, 'Le camp et la notion de vie', ibid., pp. 68–76; Federico Rahola, 'La forme-camp. Pour une généalogie des lieux de transit et d'internement du présent', *Cultures & Conflits*, 68, 2007, 32–50.

4 Hannah Arendt, *The Origins of Totalitarianism*, Cleveland, OH: Meridian, 1958, p. 284.

5 Ulrich Beck and Nina Glick Schiller have very well described and criticized the 'methodological nationalism' of sociological theory. Here we continue this critique by applying it in a general manner to political thought and the 'treatment' of foreigners in the contemporary world.

6 The work of Zygmunt Bauman is pervaded by this attempt to understand the contemporary and contradictory developments of globalization, when the excluding forces produce 'human refuse' and make the possibility of making a world on the planetary scale ever more difficult. See, in particular, *Wasted Lives: Modernity and its Outcasts*, Cambridge: Polity, 2004, and 'Des symptômes en quête d'un objet et d'un nom', in *L'Age de la régression*, Paris: Premier Parallèle, 2017.

7 See Maël Galisson, 'Voir Calais et mourir', *Plein droit* 2/2016, 109, 10–14.

8 Voir Babels, *La Mort aux frontières de l'Europe: compter, identifier, commémorer* (ed. Carolina Kobelinsky and Stefan Le Courant), Lyon: Éditions du Passager Clandestin, 2017.

9 See the documentary by Michel Agier and Nicolas Autheman, *Vicente*, Minimum Moderne/Babels, 2017: http://anrbabels.hypotheses.org/163

10 Hannah Arendt, *Qu'est-ce que la politique*, Paris: Seuil, 1995, p. 146.

11 See Marielle Macé, *Sidérer, considérer. Migrants en France*, Lagrasse: Éditions Verdier, 2017.

Index